Rachel Walter Hinkle Shoemaker

Delsartean Pantomimes with Recital and Musical Accompaniment

Designed for Home, School, and Church Entertainments

Rachel Walter Hinkle Shoemaker

Delsartean Pantomimes with Recital and Musical Accompaniment
Designed for Home, School, and Church Entertainments

ISBN/EAN: 9783337004286

Printed in Europe, USA, Canada, Australia, Japan

Cover: Foto ©ninafisch / pixelio.de

More available books at **www.hansebooks.com**

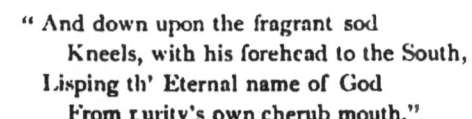

" And down upon the fragrant sod
   Kneels, with his forehead to the South,
Lisping th' Eternal name of God
   From purity's own cherub mouth."

Delsartean Pantomimes

WITH

Recital and Musical Accompaniment

DESIGNED FOR

HOME, SCHOOL, AND CHURCH ENTERTAINMENTS

BY

MRS. J. W. SHOEMAKER

"Association's mystic power combines,
Internal passions with external signs."—*Lloyd.*

Copyright, 1891, by The Penn Publishing Company

TO ALL

WHO HAVE BEEN MY PUPILS,

IN

GRATEFUL REMEMBRANCE OF THEIR KINDNESS AND OF

THEIR ENTHUSIASM IN

THAT WHICH PERTAINS TO THE BEAUTIFUL

ART OF EXPRESSION,

THIS

LITTLE VOLUME IS AFFECTIONATELY INSCRIBED.

CONTENTS

	PAGE
INTRODUCTION AND KEY TO PANTOMIMES,	11
DIAGRAM OF BASIC POSITIONS,	13

THE PANTOMIMES:

PARADISE AND THE PERI,	*Moore,*	20
THE DIVER,	*From Schiller, by Bulwer,*	41
FLAG OF THE RAINBOW,	*English,*	63
SONG OF THE MYSTIC,	*Ryan,*	71
PAUL REVERE'S RIDE,	*Longfellow,*	82
THE FAMINE,	"	96
THE BACHELOR'S SALE,	*Anon.,*	110
QUEEN VASHTI'S LAMENT,	*Reade,*	118
THE VOICE OF SPRING,	*Hemans,*	132
THE RAVEN,	*Poe,*	149

PREFACE

The increasing demand for novel entertainments, of a character elevating and æsthetic, has led to the preparation of this book.

A pure pantomime is that in which the action of the piece or play is rendered by gesticulation only.

A musical pantomime is one wherein a musical accompaniment is connected with the visible representation.

The pure pantomime was a pastime among the Greeks and Romans for many years, and it is recorded that entire plays were performed without an uttered word; while it was a matter of controversy between Cicero and Roscius as to whether the former could make the greater impression by his oratory, or the latter by his acting. Pantomime, with musical accompaniment, has been in use among the Chinese, Persians, and other Oriental people from the oldest times.

We believe that in our day and in our country, the pantomime is best received and most enjoyed where there are both recital of words and musical accompaniment, and with such end in view, these pantomimes have been thus arranged, but, if preferred, either one or both can be omitted.

Believing also that "the poetry of motion and grace of action" may find in the Pantomimic Art that full manifestation of expression which in such form it deserves to have, and trusting that this opinion is in harmony with that of the intelligent public, this little work is respectfully submitted by

THE AUTHOR.

PHILADELPHIA, July 1st, 1891.

INTRODUCTION AND KEY TO THE PANTOMIMES

Artistic effect and Truth in Expression constitute the Pantomimic Art.

To secure these it will be necessary for the amateur to *study carefully* the following explanations, and give due attention to certain preliminary exercises. By this method, the whole plan of execution of any of these Pantomimes can be readily traced, and the result will be accordingly satisfactory. The explanations are given in the briefest and plainest manner in order that the mind may have the least possible to remember, and a little care at the beginning will save much perplexity in the end.

DIAGRAM OF BASIC POSITIONS

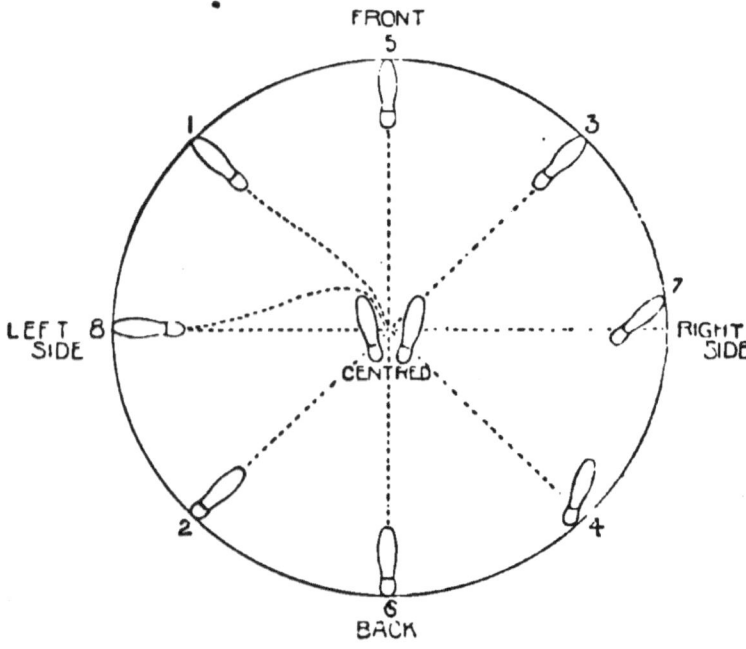

NOTE.—Some one of the above-named foot-positions is always used in the following pantomimes.

In practicing the foot-positions as indicated above, first, stand centred—that is, heels parallel and near together, equal balance in both legs, toes outward, at an angle of about sixty degrees. In making the basic changes, the *left* foot should always be kept centred, moving only off heel to toe, and inward and outward, in a pivotal way, sufficient to accommodate the fluency of movement of the right foot. As the right foot takes the various positions, the *line of gravity*, or *weight of body*, should shift into *right* leg, and this manner should be observed in *all the foot-action* of the pantomimes, unless *otherwise indicated*. Again, the foot should be raised only sufficiently to permit it escaping the floor, and it should move with an easy, pendulous action and not be jerked nor plunged, and the basic positions, whether standing in the lengths or widths, should be *strong*, otherwise the body manifestation will lack expression.

First Exercise

Position 1. Right foot diagonally front and beyond left foot. Return to centre.

Position 2. Right foot diagonally back and beyond left foot. Return to centre.

Position 3. Right foot diagonally forward—right. Return to centre.

Position 4. Right foot diagonally backward—right. Return to centre.

Position 5. Right foot directly forward. Return to centre.

Position 6. Right foot directly backward. Return to centre.

Position 7. Right foot directly to right side. Return to centre.

Position 8. Right foot over left foot to left side. Return to centre.

SECOND EXERCISE

1. From centre to position 1.
2. From position 1 direct to position 2.
3. From position 2 direct to position 3.
4. From position 3 direct to position 4.
5. From position 4 direct to position 5.
6. From position 5 direct to position 6.
7. From position 6 direct to position 7.
8. From position 7 direct to position 8.

THE ARMS

As another preliminary, there should be careful drill in the movements of the arms; swaying them slowly in and out, and up and down, describing arcs and parts of arcs with lissome, willowy motion.

All arm movements in the Pantomimes, unless otherwise specified, should be *long* and *full*, that is—all the arm levers should be brought into action, and, unless specified, the movements always *executed* in *curves*.

For convenience of *description* of the arm movements in the Pantomimes, the word *Zone* has been used with the following significance: Movements by which the hands are carried upward, from any point above the shoulder, are designated as in upper zone, those downward, from any point below the hips, as in lower zone, and those from chest outward, between shoulder and hip, as in middle zone.

Again; Arm Directions, from front to back in *any* zone are designated as follows :

Arms carried forward—Front.

Arms carried forward between front and side—Oblique—Front, either right or left.

Arms carried out to either side—Lateral.

Arms carried backward from side—Oblique—Back, either right or left.

Hand Positions

Hand positions are designated as follows:

Hand, palm upward—that is, away from earth—Palm Supine.

Hand, palm downward—that is, toward earth—Palm Prone.

Hand, palm away from body—that is, back of hand toward face—Palm Vertical.

The palm is not flatly up in supine, nor flatly down in prone, but in each case on an incline of about thirty degrees from the horizontal. Many other hand positions occur in the pantomimes, but, as each has its own special significance, they need not be mentioned here.

Transitions

Transitions or changes of *hand* positions, through arm movements are made *simultaneously* with *Basic* changes, unless no basic change is designated, in which case the former basic position is retained, and the arms themselves, or arms with upper part of body, pass by transition into the next gesture or series of gestures.

THE FACE

The face must reflect promptly and truly the varying changes of thought and emotion, and to that end there should be made a careful analysis of the selection, and the lines memorized and studied by both *pupils* and *instructor* before any part of it is taught in pantomime. If the facial expression is wanting much of the effect is lost.

NUMBER TAKING PART

Any number of ladies or girls may take part in a pantomime—limiting only in regard to extent of stage, as each pantomimist should have the allotment of at least four feet square of platform space. Care should be taken to select such persons as are naturally graceful and who will enter into the spirit of the tableaux.

THE RECITER

The reciter should, if possible, be the instructor, if not, then some one who possesses a well-modulated voice, and who will, through *spoken* language, convey the spirit of the sentiment to the ear of the hearer. Much depends upon the reciter, for it is upon the movements of the voice that the unanimity of the pantomimic action hangs. The reciter's place in the performance should be in front of the centre of the group, or to one side of it. He or she should not take any part in the action, and should study to sustain or hold the voice where long pauses are necessary for the movements of the class, and to speak with rapidity where quick changes of position occur.

THE MUSIC

The music should in all cases be sufficiently subdued to permit the reciter being distinctly heard, but in studying the adaptation, it will be found that some parts will necessarily need to be more subdued than others. The music may be selected from one or from several compositions as may seem best suited to the pantomime. The instrument, a piano or organ, should be distant from the reciter, so that the voice may not be disturbed by the notes of the instrument. Care must be exercised to have the *recital*, the *music*, and the *movements* all in *harmony*.

THE DRESS

The dress may be of any soft material from cheesecloth to flexible silk, and in color, white or cream, or any pleasing tint. It should be loose and flowing, but without train, as the latter will interfere with the placing of the feet. The Greek costume, or a modification of it, is to be preferred, as it not only gives freedom, but is in itself graceful and so facilitates grace of motion on the part of the performer.

THE LIGHTS

During the time of the performance the audience-room should be darkened, so that the light may be concentrated upon the stage. To heighten the effect, colored lights, if desired, may be thrown at intervals upon those taking part.

NOTE.—Considerable practice is necessary to produce good effect. Only two or three verses should be practiced at each hour rehearsal, and those should be gone over and over again. When the attitudes of any one poem have been learned, then the entire pantomime should be practiced for harmony and artistic effect. No musical accompaniment should be used until in the last hours of drill work.

PARADISE AND THE PERI
ADAPTED

The Peri are mythologically represented as descendants of fallen angels, excluded from Paradise until, through some holy deed, their penance is accomplished. In this instance a Peri is described as having twice appeared at the Gate of Heaven, bearing the first time a drop of blood from the heart of an expiring warrior; the second time a farewell sigh from the lips of a dying lover. In each case she is refused admission—the gift not being deemed sufficiently worthy—the angel bids her seek again, and this time she bears to Heaven a tear of repentance from the eye of a hardened sinner.

One morn a Peri at the gate
Of Eden stood, disconsolate;
And as she listened to the springs
   Of life within, like music flowing,
And caught the light upon her wings
   Through the half-open portal glowing,
She wept to think her recreant race
Should e'er have lost that glorious place!

"How happy," exclaimed this child of air,
"Are the holy spirits who wander there,
   'Mid flowers that never shall fade or fall!
Though mine are the gardens of earth and sea,
   One blossom of Heaven outblooms them all!"

The glorious angel who was keeping
The gates of light, beheld her weeping;
And, as he nearer drew and listened,
A tear within his eyelids glistened.—

" And as she listened to the springs
Of life within, like music flowing."

"Nymph of a fair but erring line!"
  Gentle he said, "one hope is thine,
  'Tis written in the book of fate,
    The Peri yet may be forgiven,
  Who brings to this eternal gate
    The gift that is most dear to Heaven!
  Go, seek it, and redeem thy sin;
  'Tis sweet to let the pardoned in!"

Rapidly as comets run
To the embraces of the sun,
Down the blue vault the Peri flies,
  And, lighted earthward by a glance
That just then broke from the morning's eyes,
  Hung hovering o'er our world's expanse.

Then over the vale of Baalbec winging
  Slowly, she sees a child at play,
Among the rosy wild-flowers singing,
  As rosy and as wild as they;
Chasing with eager hands and eyes,
The beautiful blue damsel-flies
That fluttered round the jasmine stems,
Like winged flowers or flying gems:
And near the boy, who, tired with play,
Now nestling 'mid the roses lay,
She saw a wearied man dismount
  From his hot steed, and on the brink
Of a small temple's rustic fount
  Impatient fling him down to drink.

Then swift his haggard brow he turned
   To the fair child, who fearless sat—
Though never yet hath day-beam burned
   Upon a brow more fierce than that—
Sullenly fierce—a mixture dire,
Like thunder-clouds of gloom and fire,
In which the Peri's eye could read
Dark tales of many a ruthless deed.

Yet tranquil now that man of crime
(As if the balmy evening time
Softened his spirit) looked and lay,
Watching the rosy infant's play;
Though still, whene'er his eye by chance
Fell on the boy's, its lurid glance
   Met that unclouded, joyous gaze,
As torches that have burnt all night
   Encounter morning's glorious rays.

But hark! the vesper call to prayer,
   As slow the orb of daylight sets,
Is rising sweetly on the air
   From Syria's thousand minarets!

The boy has started from the bed
Of flowers, where he had laid his head,
And down upon the fragrant sod
   Kneels, with his forehead to the south,
Lisping th' eternal name of God
   From purity's own cherub mouth;

And looking, while his hands and eyes
Are lifted to the glowing skies,
Like a stray babe of paradise,
Just lighted on that flowery plain,
And seeking for its home again!

And how felt he, the wretched man
Reclining there—while memory ran
O'er many a year of guilt and strife
That marked the dark flood of his life,
Nor found one sunny resting-place,
Nor brought him back one branch of grace?—
"There was a time," he said, in mild,
Heart-humbled tones, "thou blessed child!
When young, and haply pure as thou,
I looked and prayed like thee; but now"—
He hung his head; each nobler aim
   And hope and feeling which had slept
From boyhood's hour, that instant came
   Fresh o'er him, and he wept—he wept!

And now! behold him kneeling there,
By the child's side in humble prayer,
While the same sunbeam shines upon
The guilty and the guiltless one,
And hyms of joy proclaim through Heaven
The triumph of a soul forgiven!

'Twas when the golden orb had set,
While on their knees they lingered yet,

There fell a light more lovely far
Than ever came from sun or star—
Upon the tear that, warm and meek,
Dewed that repentant sinner's cheek:
To mortal eye this light might seem
A northern flash or meteor beam;
But well th' enraptured Peri knew
'Twas a bright smile the angel threw
From Heaven's gate, to hail that tear—
Her harbinger of glory near!
"And see!" she cried, "the crystal bar
Of Eden moves!
Joy! joy! Forever! my task is done—
The gates are passed and Heaven is won!"

THOMAS MOORE.

THE PANTOMIME

ATTITUDE

1

"One morn a Peri at the gate
Of Eden stood disconsolate:"

Stand centred—body slightly depressed—head and eyes dropped—expression mournful—hands hanging at arm's length, with loosely interlocked fingers—lower zone—front.

2

"And as she listened to the springs
Of life within, like music flowing,"

Pos. 3. Hands crossing in front—right hand passing into upper zone, near ear, as in a listening attitude—left hand into lower zone lateral—palm prone—eyes raised and oblique forward—left—chin upward.

3

"And caught the light upon her wings
Through the half open portal glowing,"

Weight of body on left foot, arms curving to front, middle zone—then right hand passing obliquely forward into upper zone, oblique right, palm vertical, left hand at same time into lower zone—lateral—extended, palm prone—head and eyes raised.

4

"She wept to think her recreant race
Should e'er have lost that glorious place:
'How happy,' exclaimed this child of air,"

Transition—hands to lower zone—front, then clasp and bring slowly to left side of neck, letting head gently rest against hands, eyes drooped, expression sad.

5

"Are the holy spirits who wander there,
'Mid flowers that never shall fade or fall!"

Head and eyes slowly raised.

6

"Though mine are the gardens of earth and sea."

Hands slowly unclasping and passing into upper zone over head, separating, and decending into lower zone, lateral, palms prone.

7

"One blossom of Heaven outblooms them all!"

Weight of body to right foot. Transition—hands carried to front, middle zone, the right crossing above the left, and passing to upper zone, oblique front, palm supine, while the left passes to lower zone, oblique back, palm prone.

" The glorious angel who was keeping
　The gates of light beheld her weeping."

Retain preceding attitude.

8

" And, as he nearer drew and listened,
　A tear within his eyelids glistened,"

Pos. 2. Transition—hands to upper zone, then outward and downward to front of waist, the right hand passing to lateral, extended, middle zone, palm prone, the left hand near left ear, in listening position, face and eyes obliquely forward to right.

9

"'Nymph of a fair but erring line!'
　Gentle he said, ' One hope is thine,
　'Tis written in the book of fate,'"

Transition—hands to middle zone, front, palms supine, face sympathetic.

10

"'The Peri yet may be forgiven,'

Slight waving movement of hands, in same position.

11

"' Who brings to this eternal gate
　The gift that is most dear to Heaven!'

Right hand carried upward and to lateral, palm supine, head and eyes following.

12

" ' Go, seek it, and redeem thy sin;
'Tis sweet to let the pardoned in!' "

Pos. 5. Transition of right hand downward and inward to chest, then to front, palm supine, head and eyes obliquely forward to left.

" Rapidly as currents run
To the embraces of the sun,"

Retain preceding attitude.

13

" Down the blue vault the Peri flies,"

Transition—hands quickly carried into upper zone, front, then outward, and downward, and inward in lower zone, making a circle, then upward again, repeating the circular motion three times, each time a little further outward on the words "*down*," "*vault*," and "*flies*," distinctively. Head forward on line with body.

14

"And, lighted earthward by a glance
That just then broke from morning's eyes;"

Hands held in middle zone, oblique front, palms prone.

15

"Hung hovering o'er the world's expanse."

Hands in same position, making three undulating upper arm movements, each time carrying the hands a little further outward.

16

"Then over the vale of Baalbec winging
Slowly, she sees a child at play,"

Hands swung slowly over to oblique front, left, then to oblique front, right, line of gravity shifting into left foot, then again into right foot, in harmony with the arm movements. On the word "sees," hands take right oblique front position, palms vertical, eyes looking forward and downward.

17

"Among the rosy wild-flowers singing,
As rosy and as wild as they,"

Fore-arm movements inward, then outward, carrying hands to same position, palms supine.

18

"Chasing with eager hands and eyes
The beautiful blue damsel-flies
That fluttered round the jasmine stems,
Like winged flowers or flying gems;"

Pos. 4. Body, and face, and toes of right foot turned

oblique—back, right, arms reaching forward, palms supine.

19

"And near the boy, who tired with play,
Now nestling 'mid the roses lay,"

Hands brought somewhat lower and nearer to body.

20

" She saw a wearied man dismount
From his hot steed, and on the brink
Of a small temple's rustic fount"

Line of gravity shifted to left foot, body retreated, head forward in same direction as preceding, but as if in scrutiny, hands oblique front, vertical, right hand a little higher than left.

"Impatient fling him down to drink;"

Pos. 1. Hands brought quickly above head, closed into fists and carried strongly by straight-line arm movements into lower zone, lateral, and held. Head firm, face impatient and looking obliquely forward over right shoulder.

21

" Then swift his haggard brow he turned
To the fair child, who fearless sat—
Though never yet hath day-beam burned
Upon a brow more fierce than that—
Sullenly fierce—a mixture dire,
Like thunder-clouds of gloom and fire,"

Arms firmly folded, eyes looking downward and forward over right shoulder, face unhappy.

22

"In which the Peri's eye could read
Dark tales of many a ruthless deed."

Pos. 2. Hand transition through upper zone, then downward and inward toward front of chest, then forward, palms vertical, body somewhat retreated.

23

"Yet tranquil now that man of crime
(As if the balmy evening time
Softened his spirit) looked and lay,
Watching the rosy infant's play
Though still where'er his eye by chance
Fell on the boy's, its lurid glance"

Position centred, line of gravity in left foot, head resting with chin in left palm, left elbow supported by right hand, countenance softened, eyes forward and downward toward oblique right.

24

"Met that unclouded joyous gaze,
As torches that have burned all night
Encounter morning's glorious rays."

Head more drooping and slowly moved toward oblique left, eyes downward; on last line, carry hands into upper zone, front, then, with slow descent, oblique front to lower zone.

25

"But hark! the vesper call to prayer,
  As slow the orb of daylight sets,"

Pos. 5. (Narrow)—Hands loosely clasping in lower zone, front, and close to body, head inclined a little forward and downward toward left, eyes looking forward and upward toward oblique right.

26

"Is rising sweetly on the air
  From Syria's thousand minarets!"

Hands rising, palms downward, into upper zone, front, and curving over into oblique front, palms supine, on second line.

27

"The boy has started from the bed
  Of flowers, where he had laid his head,
  And down upon the fragrant sod"

Hand transition inward, then outward in upper zone, on second line, then floating downward into lower zone, on third line; as the hands are descending, slowly sink downward upon left knee.

28

"Kneels with his forehead to the south,
  Lisping the eternal name of God
  From purity's own cherub mouth;"

Hands crossed upon chest, head bowed, whole manner reverent.

29

"And looking while his hands and eyes
Are lifted to the glowing skies,
Like a stray babe of paradise."

Hands slowly unfolding and passing into upper zone, front, palms supine, head and eyes raised, whole manner devotional.

30

"Just lighted on that flowery plain,
And seeking for its home again."

Hands curving outward and slowly descending, palms prone, at the same time body slowly rising, recover position, placing line of gravity in left foot.

31

"And how felt he, the wretched man
Reclining there—while memory ran
O'er many a year of guilt and strife
That marked the dark flood of his life,
Nor found one sunny resting place,
Nor brought him back one branch of grace!—
'There was a time,' he said, in mild,
Heart-humbled tones, 'thou blessed child
When young, and haply pure as thou,

Head down, oblique left, face dejected, hands tightly clasping each other in lower zone, front.

32

"'I looked and prayed like thee; but now'—

Hands still clasped but carried up on chest, elbows

thrown outward and upward, face expressive of strong emotion, head and eyes raised.

33
" He hung his head; each nobler aim
And hope and feeling which had slept
From boyhood's hour, that instant came
Fresh o'er him, and he wept—he wept!"

Line of gravity in right foot, hands still clasped but carried a few inches from chest, head dropped with forehead resting upon clasped hands, elbows well out.

34
"And now! behold him kneeling there,
By the child's side in humble prayer,"

Hand transition to upper zone, front, outward and downward, in toward chest, then forward to oblique front, right, palms vertical, eyes oblique right, forward and downward, whole manner interested.

35
" While the same sunbeam shines upon
The guilty and the guiltless one,"

Hand transition from middle zone, front, left hand passing to lower zone, lateral, extended, palm prone, right hand to upper zone, oblique front, palm vertical, then slowly descending into lower zone, on the words "shines upon," etc.

36

"And hymns of joy proclaim through Heaven"

Hand transition from lower zone, front, into upper zone, oblique front, palms supine.

37

"The triumph of a soul forgiven!"

Pos. 1. Body strongly up, hand transition, upper zone, front, left hand carried directly above head, finger-tips upward, right hand passing outward to lower zone, lateral, palm prone.

38

"'Twas when the golden orb had set,
While on their knees they lingered yet,"

Pos. 6. (Narrow)—Hand transition from upper zone, outward and into lower zone, front, then coming up in front of chest and placed palm to palm, finger-tips upward, elbows outward, at same time sink slowly to floor upon right knee, face and eyes raised, as in adoration, retain this attitude through following lines:

> "There fell a light more lovely far
> Than ever came from sun or star
> Upon the tear that, warm and meek,
> Dewed that repentant sinner's cheek;
> To mortal eye its light might seem
> A northern flash or meteor beam."

39

"But well th' enraptured Peri knew
'Twas a bright smile the angel threw
From Heaven's gate, to hail that tear—
Her harbinger of glory near!"

Rise to Pos. 5, at same time hands carried quickly to upper zone, front, then outward, downward, inward, then crossed upon chest, head and eyes upward, face radiant.

40

"'And see,' she cried, 'the crystal bar
Of Eden moves!'"

Pos. 6. Hands thrown into upper zone over head, palms well open, facing front.

41

"'Joy! joy forever! My task is done—
The gates are passed and Heaven is won!'"

Pos. 5. Body raised to utmost, hand transition, outward, downward and upward, making two complete circles on the words "joy! joy forever!" then outward in upper zone, lateral, palms vertical on the words "the gates are passed," then downward, and again circling into upper zone, front, and held to end of lines, palm of right hand upward, palm of left hand downward, finger-tips of one hand nearly touching those of the other.

"Ah! father, my father, what more can there rest?
 Enough of this sport with the pitiless ocean—
He has served you as none would thyself hast confessed."

THE DIVER

FROM THE GERMAN OF SCHILLER BY BULWER
ABRIDGED

" Oh ! where is the knight or the squire so bold
 As to dive to the howling Charybdis below ?—
I cast in the whirlpool a goblet of gold,
 And o'er it already the dark waters flow;
Whoever to me may the goblet bring,
Shall have for his guerdon that gift of his king."

He spoke, and the cup from the terrible steep,
 That, rugged and hoary, hung over the verge
Of the endless and measureless world of the deep,
 Twirled into the maelstrom that maddened the surge.
" And where is the diver so stout to go—
I ask ye again—to the deep below?"

And the knights and the squires that gathered around,
 Stood silent—and fixed on the ocean their eyes;
They looked on the dismal and savage Profound,
 And the peril chilled back every thought of the prize.
And thrice spoke the monarch—" The cup to win,
Is there never a wight who will venture in ?"

And all, as before, heard in silence the king,
 Till a youth with an aspect unfearing but gentle,
'Mid the tremulous squires—stepped out from the ring.

Unbuckling his girdle, and doffing his mantle;
And the murmuring crowd, as they parted asunder,
On the stately boy cast their looks of wonder.

As he strode to the marge of the summit, and gave
   One glance on the gulf of that merciless main,
Lo! the wave that forever devours the wave,
   Casts roaringly up the Charybdis again;
And, as with the swell of the far thunder-boom,
Rushes foamingly forth from the heart of the gloom.

The youth gave his trust to his Maker! Before
   That path through the riven abyss closed again,
Hark! a shriek from the gazers that circle the shore—
   And, behold! he is whirled in the grasp of the main!
And o'er him the breakers mysteriously rolled,
And the giant mouth closed on the swimmer so bold.

All was still on the height, save the murmur that went
   From the grave of the deep, sounding hollow and fell,
Or save when the tremulous sighing lament
   Thrilled from lip unto lip,—" Gallant youth, fare thee well!"
More hollow and more wails the deep on the ear—
More dread and more dread grows suspense in its fear.

And, lo! from the heart of that far-floating gloom,
   Like the wing of the cygnet—what gleams on the sea?
Lo! an arm and a neck glancing up from the tomb!
   Steering stalwart and shoreward. O joy, it is he!

The left hand is lifted in triumph; behold,
It waves as a trophy the goblet of gold!

And he comes, with the crowd in their clamor and glee;
    And the goblet his daring has won from the water,
He lifts to the king as he sinks on his knee—
    And the king from her maidens has beckoned his daughter.
She pours to the boy the bright wine which they bring,
And thus spoke the Diver—" Long life to the King!

" Happy they whom the rose-hues of daylight rejoice,
    The air and the sky that to mortals are given!
May the horror below never more find a voice—
    Nor man stretch too far the wide mercy of Heaven!
Nevermore, nevermore may he lift from the sight
The veil which is woven with terror and night!

" Quick brightening like lightning, the ocean rushed o'er me,
    Wild floating, borne down fathom-deep from the day;
Till a torrent rushed out on the torrents that bore me,
    And doubled the tempest that whirled me away.
Vain, vain was my struggle—the circle had won me,
Round and round in its dance the mad element spun me.

" From the deep, then I called upon God, and He heard me,
    In the dread of my need, He vouchsafed to mine eye
A rock jutting out from the grave that interred me;

I sprung there, I clung there, and death passed me by,
And, lo! where the goblet gleamed through the abyss,
By a coral reef saved from the far Fathomless.

" Below, at the foot of that precipice drear,
    Spread the gloomy, and purple, and pathless Obscure!
A silence of horror that slept on the ear,
    That the eye more appalled might the horror endure!
Salamander, snake, dragon—vast reptiles that dwell
In the deep—coiled about the grim jaws of their hell.

" Methought, as I gazed through the darkness, that now
    I saw a dread hundred-limbed creature—its prey!—
And darted, devouring; I sprang from the bough
    Of the coral, and swept on the horrible way;
And the whirl of the mighty wave seized me once more,
It seized me to save me, and dash to the shore."

On the youth gazed the monarch, and marvelled: quoth
    he,
" Bold diver, the goblet I promised is thine;
And this ring I will give, a fresh guerdon to thee—
    Never jewels more precious shone up from the mine—
If thou'lt bring me fresh tidings, and venture again,
To say what lies hid in the innermost main!"

Then out spake the daughter in tender emotion—
    " Ah! father, my father, what more can there rest?
Enough of this sport with the pitiless ocean—
    He has served thee as none would, thyself hast confessed.

If nothing can slake thy wild thirst of desire,
Let thy knights put to shame the exploit of the squire!"

The king seized the goblet, he swung it on high,
    And whirling, it fell in the roar of the tide:
" But bring back that goblet again to my eye,
    And I'll hold thee the dearest that rides by my side;
And thine arms shall embrace, as thy bride, I decree,
The maiden whose pity now pleadeth for thee."

And heaven, as he listened, spoke out from the space,
    And the hope that makes heroes shot flame from his eyes;
He gazed on the blush in that beautiful face—
    It pales—at the feet of her father she lies!
How priceless the guerdon! a moment—a breath—
And headlong he plunges to life and to death!

They hear the loud surges sweep back in their swell;
    Their coming the thunder-sound heralds along!
Fond eyes yet are tracking the spot where he fell—
    They come the wild waters in tumult and throng,
Roaring up to the cliff, roaring back as before;
But no wave ever brought the lost youth to the shore.

THE PANTOMIME

ATTITUDE

1

"'Oh! where is the knight or the squire so bold
 As to dive to the howling Charybdis below?'"
Pos 1. Right hand in middle zone, front, palm supine, left hand down near side, eyes looking toward oblique front, left.

2

"'I cast in the whirlpool a goblet of gold,
 And o'er it already the dark waters flow;'"
Right hand passing in toward chest, then to upper zone, over head, palm upward.

3

"'Whoever to me may the goblet bring,
 Shall have for his guerdon that gift of his king.'"
Hand position same as in first attitude.

4

"He spoke, and the cup from the terrible steep,
 That, rugged and hoary, hung over the verge
 Of the endless and measureless world of the deep,"
Pos. 5. Right hand to same position as in attitude second, but higher and stronger.

5

"Twirled into the maelstrom that maddened the surge."

Right hand descending to middle zone, front, then describing three inward circling wrist-motions on "twirled into the maelstrom," then held with palm prone on remainder of the line.

6

"'And where is the diver so stout to go—
I ask ye again—to the deep below?'"

Line of gravity to left foot. Transition—hands pass to middle zone front, right crossing above left, then both to oblique front, palms supine, eyes again to oblique left.

7

"And the knights and the squires that gathered around,
  Stood silent—and fixed on the ocean their eyes;
They looked on the dismal and savage Profound,
  And the peril chilled back every thought of the prize.
And thrice spoke the monarch—'The cup to win,
Is there never a wight who will venture in?'
And all, as before, heard in silence the king,
  Till a youth with an aspect unfearing but gentle,"

Pos. 6. (Narrow) Transition—hands passing into upper zone, then floating outward and downward, and inward, then arms folded, eyes looking forward and downward, face thoughtful.

8

"'Mid the tremulous squires stepped out from the ring."

Pos. 5. Face front.

9

"Unbuckling his girdle and doffing his mantle;"

Transition—hands passing into upper zone, then outward and downward, and inward to front of waist on "Unbuckling," and quickly up to shoulders on "Doffing," then floating outward and downward.

10

"And the murmuring crowd, as they parted asunder,
On the stately boy cast their looks of wonder,
As he strode to the marge of the summit, and gave
    One glance on the gulf of that merciless main."

Line of gravity to left foot. Transition—hands curving inward from preceding descending motion, to middle zone front, and outward to oblique front, palms vertical, and retained. Eyes anxious, but interested.

11

"Lo! the wave that forever devours the wave,
    Casts roaringly up the Charybdis again;"

Line of gravity to right foot. Transition—hands passing inward toward each other, then outward and into upper zone, oblique front, palms vertical and retained.

12

"And, as with the swell of the far thunder-boom,
Rushes foamingly forth from the heart of the gloom."

Hands swept downward and over to left lateral, middle zone on "Swell," then curving over to oblique front, right, on "Rushes foamingly forth."

13

"The youth gave his trust to his Maker!"

Hands slowly passing down to side, eyes raised.

14

"Before that path through the riven abyss closed again,"

Right hand carried near chest, palm vertical, eyes looking forward and downward.

15

"Hark! A shriek from the gazers that circle the shore—"

Line of gravity to left foot, body slightly retreated, left hand carried to upper zone a few inches from left ear, and right hand into upper zone in front and above head, palm vertical, elbows well out.

16

"And, behold! he is whirled in the grasp of the main!"

Line of gravity to right foot. Transition—hands to lower zone front, then to upper zone, oblique front, palms vertical on "Behold," and retained.

17

"And o'er him the breakers mysteriously rolled,
And the giant mouth closed on the swimmer so bold.

All was still on the height, save the murmur that went
　From the grave of the deep, sounding hollow and
　　fell,"

Hands slowly descending on first line, then curving inward and outward, and downward on " Closed."

18

" Or save when the tremulous sighing lament,
　Thrilled from lip unto lip—' Gallant youth, fare thee
　　well!' "

Hands carried very slowly to front of chest and clasped, elbows well out, face sympathetic.

19

" More hollow and more wails the deep on the ear,
More dread and more dread grows suspense in its fear.
And, lo! from the heart of that far-floating gloom,
　Like the wing of a cygnet—what gleams on the sea?
Lo! an arm and a neck glancing up from the tomb!
　Steering stalwart and shoreward."

Pos. 3. Transition—hands unclasping and rising into upper zone, then outward and downward into middle zone, the right coming inward and held over brow on third line, left hand at same time descending into lower zone, near side, eyes looking anxiously forward, oblique right.

20

" O joy, it is he!"

Line of gravity to left foot, hands waved above head, expression joyous.

21

"The left hand is lifted in triumph; behold,"

Line of gravity to right foot. Transition—hands passing outward and downward into middle zone, then in near waist, right curving above left, and carried at full arm's length over head, palm facing front, left at same time passing downward to left near side, face front and exultant.

22

"It waves as a trophy the goblet of gold!"

Right hand describing three inward waving motions over head.

23

"And he comes, with the crowd in their clamor and glee,
And the goblet his daring has won from the water,"

Line of gravity to left foot. Transition—hands passing to middle zone front, one crossing above the other, then both to oblique front, palms supine.

24

"He lifts to the king as he sinks on his knee,
And the king from her maidens has beckoned his
    daughter,
And she pours to the boy the bright wine which they
    bring,
And thus spoke the Diver:

Sink to floor on left knee. Transition—hands passing inward near front of chest, right crossing above left and moving to extended front, somewhat in upper zone, palm supine, left passing inward and placed upon chest, face upward.

25
" 'Long life to the King!'

Rise to feet, line of gravity in left foot, right hand passing in near lips, then forward, and outward, and downward to side.

26
"' Happy they whom the rose-hues of daylight rejoice,
The air and the sky that to mortals are given!'

Eyes raised.

27
"' May the horror below **nevermore** find a voice '—

Head downward and moved negatively on "nevermore."

28
" 'Nor man stretch too far the wide mercy of Heaven!'

Transition—hands passing into upper zone, front, then outward and downward to middle zone, lateral, palms prone, head up.

29
"'Nevermore, nevermore may he lift from the sight
The veil which is woven with terror and night!'

Transition—hands passing inward from lateral to front, the right to upper zone, front, palm vertical, and left to lower zone, near side, palm prone, face and eyes turned toward oblique back, left.

30

"'Quick brightening like lightning, the ocean rushed o'er me,'

Transition—hands moving into upper zone, then outward and downward and crossing each other near waist, then outward to front, palms prone on "ocean rushed o'er me," face toward oblique left.

31

"'Wild floating, borne down fathom-deep from the day;

Hands moving inward, then forward to lower zone, front, palms facing each other.

32

"'Till a torrent rushed out on the torrents that bore me,'

Hands moving inward and upward to oblique front, upper zone, palms vertical.

33

"'And doubled the tempest that whirled me away. Vain, vain was my struggle—the circle had won me,'

Line of gravity to right foot, transition—both hands passing to middle zone, lateral, right, and strongly extended, palms prone, head in same direction as hands.

34

" 'Round and round in its dance the mad element spun me.'

Transition—hands passing to middle zone, front, then describing three full circles by inward, and upward, and outward movements on the utterance of the line.

35

" 'From the deep, then I called upon God, and He heard me,
In the dread of my need, He vouchsafed to mine eye'

Line of gravity to left foot. Transition—hands descending low in middle zone, oblique front, palms prone, eyes raised.

36

" 'A rock jutting out from the grave that interred me,'

Line of gravity to right foot. Transition—hands moving to front, right crossing above left, then out to oblique front, right, on "rock," index finger leading, left hand at same time moving to lower zone near side, palm prone.

37

" 'I sprung there, I clung there, and death passed me by,'

Transition—hands passed quickly into middle zone, left, lateral, then quickly forward to upper zone, oblique front, right, palms vertical, head and body in same line.

38

"'And, lo! where the goblet gleamed through the abyss,
By a coral reef saved from the far Fathomless.'

Transition—hands pass to middle zone, front, right crossing above left to oblique front, and low in middle zone, index finger pointing, the left hand at the same time passes out to lateral, high in lower zone, palm prone, head and eyes turned to oblique front, right.

39

"' Below, at the foot of that precipice drear,
Spread the gloomy, and purple, and pathless Obscure!
A silence of horror that slept on the ear,
That the eye more appalled might the horror endure!
Salamander, snake, dragon—vast reptiles that dwell
In the deep—coiled about the grim jaws of their hell.
Methought, as I gazed through the darkness, that now'

Transition—hands passing inward toward chest, then outward to oblique front, right, right arm most extended, palms nearly prone, eyes looking downward and forward, oblique right, body slightly retreated, retain position to end of lines.

40

"'I saw a dread hundred-limbed creature—its prey!
And darted, devouring!'

Line of gravity to left foot, body retreated, hands into

upper zone, over head, palms vertical, elbows outward, face expressive of terror; looking forward and downward, oblique right.

41

"'I sprang from the bough,
   Of the coral, and swept on the horrible way!'

Transition—hands carried over to right side and then swept to left side, well extended, middle zone, palms prone, eyes in same direction.

42

"'And the whirl of the mighty wave seized me once
   more,
It seized me to save me, and dash to the shore.'

Body easily erect. Transition—hands carried to upper zone over head and slowly descending to side, eyes looking front.

43

" On the youth gazed the monarch, and marveled: quoth
   he,
'Bold diver, the goblet I promised is thine.'

Line of gravity to left foot, body turned slightly to oblique left, arms folded, right above left, face interested.

44

"'And this ring I will give, a fresh guerdon to thee—
Never jewels more precious shone up from the mine—

If thou'lt bring me fresh tidings, and venture again,
To say what lies hid in the innermost main!'"

Right hand rises a few inches above left elbow and remains not far from left chest, thumbs and index finger appearing to hold a ring, palm facing chest.

45

"Then out spake the daughter in tender emotion—
'Ah! father, my father, what more can there rest?
Enough of this sport with the pitiless ocean—
He has served thee as none would, thyself hast confessed,
If nothing can slack thy wild thirst of desire,
Let thy knights put to shame the exploit of the squire!'"

On first line pass to Pos. 2, hands rising into upper zone, then passing outward and downward and inward to chest and clasped on second line—at same time sink to floor on right knee, body turned directly toward right, hands remaining clasped but carried to arm's length forward, and held low, in upper zone, head and eyes raised.

46

"The king seized the goblet,"

Rise quickly to Pos. 7, hands at same time passing over head, making transition by crossing in front of chest, the right rising to utmost above head, the left to lower zone near side, face front, whole manner animated.

47
"He swung it on high,"

Describe two inward circles with right hand over head.

48
"And whirling, it fell in the roar of the tide:"

Right hand vigorously descending to lower zone, oblique front on "Fell," eyes following.

49
"'But bring back that goblet again to my eye,'

Line of gravity to left foot. Transition—right hand toward left shoulder, then to oblique front, right, lower zone, palm supine, face turned oblique left.

50
"'And I'll hold thee the dearest that rides by my side,'

Right hand carried round toward left, index finger pointing toward left side.

51
"'And thine arms shall embrace as thy bride, I decree, The maiden whose pity now pleadeth for thee.'"

Pos. 6. Right hand carried oblique back, right, lower

zone, palm supine, eyes in same direction and downward on "Maiden."

52

"And heaven, as he listened, spoke out from the space,"

Transition—hands passing to lower zone front, near body, and strongly clasped, eyes raised.

53

"And the hope that makes heroes shot flame from his eyes."

Eyes looking front, body well drawn up.

54

"He gazed on the blush in that beautiful face,
It pales—at the feet of her father she lies!"

Head turned oblique—back, right, eyes looking downward.

55

"How priceless the guerdon! a moment—a breath—"

Transition—hands to upper zone, then outward, and downward and inward toward chest on "A moment—a breath."

56

"And headlong he plunges to life and to death."

Pos. 3. Hands to upper zone, oblique, right, forward, palms vertical.

57

"They hear the loud surges sweep back in their swell;
Their coming the thunder-sound heralds along,"

Line of gravity to left foot. Transition—hands passing inward, then over and above head, eyes oblique right, looking forward and downward.

58

"Fond eyes yet are tracking the spot where he fell—
They come, the wild waters, in tumult and throng,"

Line of gravity to right foot. Right hand carried to upper zone, oblique right, above head, palm vertical, left out at left side, palm prone.

59

"Rearing up to the cliff, roaring back as before,"

Transition—hands carried by long curving sweep to left on "Rearing," then to right on "Roaring."

60

"But no wave ever brought the lost youth to the shore."

Line of gravity to left foot. Transition—hands slowly passing up over head, then outward and downward to side, head and eyes looking downward, front.

"While but a man is alive to defend it."
Flag of the Rainbow and Banner of Stars."

FLAG OF THE RAINBOW

Flag of the rainbow, and banner of stars,
   Emblem of light, and shield of the lowly,
Never to droop while our soldiers and tars
   Rally to guard it from outrage unholy.
Never may shame or misfortune attend it,
Enmity sully, or treachery rend it,
While but a man is alive to defend it:
   Flag of the rainbow, and banner of stars.

Flag of a land where the people are free,
   Ever the breezes salute and caress it;
Planted on earth, or afloat on the sea,
   Gallant men guard it, and fair women bless it.
Fling out its folds o'er a country united,
Warmed by the fires that our forefathers lighted,
Refuge where down-trodden man is invited:
   Flag of the rainbow, and banner of stars.

Flag that our sires gave in trust to their sons,
   Symbol and sign of a liberty glorious,
While the grass grows and the clear water runs,
   Ever invincible, ever victorious.
Long may it 'waken our pride and devotion,
Rippling its colors in musical motion,
First on the land, and supreme on the ocean:
   Flag of the rainbow, and banner of stars.

THOMAS DUNN ENGLISH

THE PANTOMIME

If desired, the dress may in some manner display the colors of the country.

Music—patriotic, but subdued.

ATTITUDE

1

" Flag of the rainbow, and banner of stars,
  Emblem of light, and shield of the lowly,
Never to droop while our soldiers and tars "

Pos. 3. (Narrow.) Line of gravity in left foot, arms folded, eyes looking forward and upward, chin raised.

2

" Rally to guard it from outrage unholy.
Never may shame or misfortune attend it,"

Pos. 6. Transition—both hands rising into upper zone, then outward and downward, right hand passing to left side as if grasping the hilt of a sword, left hand clinched and lateral, extended in lower zone, expression earnest.

3

" Enmity sully, or treachery rend it,"

Transition—hands carried to upper zone, then to middle zone, oblique front, palms prone on " enmity sully," then both inward toward chest, then outward to lower zone, lateral, straight line movement, hands closed in fist, muscles well tensioned.

4

" While but a man is alive to defend it:"

Pos. 5. Transition—right hand in fist to left side, then, by straight line movement, to upper zone, oblique front, right, thumb part of hand upward as if holding a sword, left hand clinched in lower zone, out at side, face strong, whole manner earnest and enthusiastic.

5

" Flag of the rainbow, and banner of stars."

Transition—hands to front, middle zone, right hand crossing above left, then to upper zone, front, palm supine, left hand to lower zone, lateral, palm prone.

6

" Flag of a land where the people are free,
  Ever the breezes salute and caress it;"

Retain same attitude on first line. Transition—on second line, hands pass inward near chest and cross one above the other, then both to upper zone, oblique front, palms vertical, waved inward then outward on "salute" and "caress," then held.

7

" Planted on earth, or afloat on the sea,"

Transition—right hand carried forward and downward by straight line movement, palm supine and strong, on "planted on earth," left hand at same time downward to side—on "afloat on the sea," right hand carried inward to left shoulder, then outward, middle zone to right, lateral, palm prone.

8

"Gallant men guard it, and fair women bless it."

Transition—hands inward toward chest, crossing one above the other, then to upper zone, oblique front, palms supine, chin up, eyes raised.

9

"Fling out its folds"

Transition—hands coming inward toward forehead, then outward, high in upper zone, oblique front, palms vertical.

10

"O'er a country united,
  Warmed by the fires that our forefathers lighted,
  Refuge where down-trodden man is invited:
  Flag of the rainbow, and banner of stars."

Transition—hands downward to middle zone, crossing in front, then to lateral, and each clasping the hand on each side of the person next, those standing on the extreme ends, raising the outer hand as in exultation—retain attitude to end of stanza.

11

"Flag that our sires gave in trust to their sons,
 Symbol and sign of a liberty glorious,
 While the grass grows and the clear water runs,"

Transition—hands inward, front, middle zone, crossing one above the other, then to oblique front, supine on the word "gave," and held, eyes front.

12

"Ever invincible,"

Body strongly drawn up. Transition—hands inward, front, right hand crossing above left, then to upper zone, high over head, index finger straight, palm facing front, left hand downward, close to side, face confident.

13

"Ever victorious!"

Transition—right hand waved strongly twice over head, eyes upward.

14

"Long may it 'waken our pride and devotion,
 Rippling its colors in musical motion,"

Transition—hands placed one upon the other high on chest on "pride and devotion," then passing into upper zone, front, and gently moving inward and outward by wrist motion on "musical motion."

15

" First on the land, and supreme on the ocean:"

Transition—right hand to middle zone, front, palm supine, left down at side on " first on the land," then right hand carried to upper zone, lateral, on " supreme," palm facing front.

16

"Flag of the rainbow, and banner of stars."

Transition—hands toward front of chest, then to upper zone, oblique front, palms supine and held to end of line.

"And I have seen Thoughts in the valley,
  'Ah! me, how my spirit was stirred!'
And they wear holy veils on their faces,
  Their footsteps can scarcely be heard."

SONG OF THE MYSTIC.

I walk down the Valley of Silence—
   Down the dim, voiceless valley—alone!
And I hear not the fall of a footstep
   Around me, save God's and my own;
And the hush of my heart is as holy
   As hovers where angels have flown!

Long ago was I weary of voices
   Whose music my heart could not win;
Long ago was I weary of noises
   That fretted my soul with their din;
Long ago was I weary of places
   Where I met but the human—and sin.

I walked in the world with the worldly;
   I craved what the world never gave;
And I said: "In the world each Ideal,
   That shines like a star on life's wave,
Is wrecked on the shores of the Real,
   And sleeps like a dream in a grave."

And still did I pine for the Perfect,
   And still found the False with the True;
I sought 'mid the Human for Heaven,
   But caught a mere glimpse of its Blue;

And I wept when the clouds of the Mortal
　　Veiled even that glimpse from my view

And I toiled on, heart-tired of the Human;
　　And I moaned 'mid the mazes of men;
Till I knelt, long ago, at an altar
　　And I heard a voice call me—since then
I walk down the Valley of Silence
　　That lies far beyond mortal ken.

Do you ask what I found in the Valley?
　　'Tis my Trysting Place with the Divine.
And I fell at the feet of the Holy,
　　And above me a voice said: "Be mine."
And there rose from the depths of my spirit
　　An echo—"My heart shall be Thine."

Do you ask how I live in the Valley?
　　I weep—and I dream—and I pray.
But my tears are as sweet as the dewdrops
　　That fall on the roses in May;
And my prayer like a perfume from Censers,
　　Ascendeth to God night and day

※　　※　　※　　※　　※　　※　　※

But far on the deep there are billows
　　That never shall break on the beach;
And I have heard songs in the Silence,
　　That never shall float into speech;
And I have had dreams in the Valley,
　　Too lofty for language to reach.

And I have seen Thoughts in the Valley—
  Ah! me, how my spirit was stirred!
And they wear holy veils on their faces,
  Their footsteps can scarcely be heard;
They pass through the Valley like Virgins,
  Too pure for the touch of a word!

Do you ask me the place of the Valley,
  Ye hearts that are harrowed by Care?
It lieth afar between mountains,
  And God and His angels are there;
And one is the dark mount of Sorrow,
  And one the bright mountain of Prayer!
FATHER RYAN

THE PANTOMIME

All movements slow, soft, and rhythmical.

ATTITUDE

1

" I walk down the Valley of Silence—"

Pos. 5—(Narrow.) Hands at side.

2

" Down the dim, voiceless valley—alone!"

Transition—right hand rising and moving in toward left chest, then outward to oblique front, right, palm supine.

3

" And I hear not the fall of a footstep "

Transition—left hand rising to middle zone, lateral, right hand to same on right, then both coming inward toward chest.

4

" Around me, save God's and my own ;"

Transition—both hands moving outward from preceding, to lateral, palms vertical, chin up, eyes raised.

5

" And the hush of my heart is as holy
As hovers where angels have flown."

Transition—hands passing downward, then inward front and placed upon heart, attitude retained.

6

"Long ago was I weary of voices
  Whose music my heart could not win;"

Pos. 6—(Narrow.) Transition—hands passing to upper zone front, then floating downward to sides, palms prone.

7

"Long ago was I weary of noises
  That fretted my soul with their din;"

Transition—right hand passing to front, middle zone, then outward to lateral, palm prone, eyes following.

8

"Long ago was I weary of places
  Where I met but the human—and sin."

Repeat same on left side, only a little stronger.

9

"I walked in the world with the worldly;"

Pos. 5. Transition—hands passing in toward chest, then outward to oblique front, palms supine.

10

"I craved what the world never gave;
  And I said: 'In the world each Ideal,'

Repeat same gesture on first line, with palms prone.

11

"'That shines like a star on life's wave,'

Transition—right hand passing in toward chest, then upward and downward to preceding position.

12

"'Is wrecked on the shores of the Real,
And sleeps like a dream in a grave.'
And still did I pine for the Perfect,
And still found the False with the True;"

Transition—both hands in toward chest, then slightly upward and outward to lower zone, lateral, palms prone, hold position to end of stanza.

13

"I sought 'mid the Human for Heaven,"

Transition—both hands passing to front of chest, crossing one above the other, then to oblique front, palms supine.

14

"But caught a mere glimpse of its Blue;"

Transition—hands crossing near chest, right hand moving to front, palm vertical and slightly moved on expression "mere glimpse," left hand floating downward to side.

15

"And I wept when the clouds of the Mortal
 Veiled even that glimpse from my view."

Transition—hands passing in toward chest, then into upper zone, oblique front, palms vertical, eyes raised.

16

"And I toiled on, heart-tired of the Human;
 And I moaned 'mid the mazes of men;"

Pos. 6—(Narrow.) Transition—hands curving inward from front oblique, then outward and floating down to side.

17

"Till I knelt, long ago, at an altar
 And I heard a voice call me—"

Pos. 5—(Narrow.) Transition—right hand passing to left chest, then to lower zone, front, palm prone, eyes following.

18

"Since then
 I walk down the Valley of Silence
 That lies far beyond mortal ken."

Transition—right hand coming in toward chest, then floating outward to middle zone, lateral, palm prone "on far beyond," then downward at side.

19

"Do you ask what I found in the Valley?
 'Tis my Trysting Place with the Divine."

Transition—hands to middle zone, front, crossing one above the other, then moving to oblique front, palms supine—on second line head and eyes raised.

20

"And I fell at the feet of the Holy,
And above me a voice said: 'Be mine.'"

Transition—hands passing outward and downward, then clasping each other in lower zone, front, near body, head bowed, appearance reverent.

21

"And there rose from the depths of my spirit
An echo—'My heart shall be Thine.'"

Body drawn upward, head slowly rising and eyes looking upward, hands placed one upon the other on chest.

22

"Do you ask how I live in the Valley?
I weep—and I dream—and I pray."

Transition—hands passing from chest and floating outward to oblique front, palms supine.

23

"But my tears are as sweet as the dewdrops
That fall on the roses in May;"

Slight repetition of preceding gesture.

24

"And my prayer like a perfume from Censers,
Ascendeth to God night and day."

Transition—hands coming toward chest, right hand crossing above left, then moving to upper zone, front, palm supine, left hand floating down to side.

* * * * * * * *

25
" But far on the deep there are billows
   That never shall break on the beach ;"

Pos. 7—(Narrow.) Transition—right hand passing downward toward left shoulder, then to middle zone, lateral right, palm prone.

26
" And I have heard songs in the Silence,
   That never shall float into speech ;"

Line of gravity to left foot, head inclined to left, right hand curving inward, then toward right ear as if listening, eyes toward oblique left and upward.

27
" And I have had dreams in the Valley,
   Too lofty for language to reach."

Transition—right hand passing outward and in toward chest, then front, index finger raised as if calling attention.

28
" And I have seen Thoughts in the Valley—
   Ah ! me, how my spirit was stirred !"

Pos. 6—(Narrow.) Transition—hands passing toward chest, then outward to oblique front, palms vertical on first line, then inward, placing palm to palm in front of chest, elbows well out, head somewhat downward, eyes drooped.

29

" And they wear holy veils on their faces,
　Their footsteps can scarcely be heard ;"

Transition—hands passing front, palms vertical, then moving a little to left, then to right, and on last line hands curving inward, then floating to lower zone, oblique front, palms prone.

30

" They pass through the Valley like Virgins,
　Too pure for the touch of a word !"

Transition—hands rising to middle zone, left oblique front, then passing in front of chest over to right lateral, palms vertical, eyes following.

31

Do you ask me the place of the Valley,
　Ye hearts that are harrowed by Care ?"

Pos. 5. Transition—hands inward toward chest, then to oblique front, palms supine, eyes front.

32

" It lieth afar between mountains,
　And God and His angels are there;"

Transition—hands crossing in front, near chest, right passing to upper zone and almost directly over head, palm facing front, left hand at same time floating slowly down to side, palm prone and held through second line.

33
"And one is the dark mount of Sorrow,"

Right hand passing inward, above head, then to oblique front, palm prone.

34
"And one the bright mountain of Prayer!"

Transition—left hand passing to front, near chest, then to upper zone, oblique front, palm supine, head and eyes raised.

(In the two following pantomimes there are noted lines 1, 2, 3, etc.—these correspond to the individual lines of the poems, and any one possessing a copy of the poems, by numbering the lines thereof, will have no difficulty in following the explanations.)

PAUL REVERE'S RIDE—Longfellow

THE PANTOMIME

ATTITUDE

1

Lines 1, 2, 3, 4, 5, 6, 7, 8, and 9:

Stand centred—fingers loosely interlocked behind back, eyes front, face cheerful, on third line look toward oblique left, and upward as if in thought; then eyes again to front, on eighth and ninth lines, look toward oblique right and upward.

2

Line 10:

Right hand passing to middle zone, front, index finger prominent for the word "one," then passing to right oblique, front, palm supine on "two," left hand hanging easily at left side, eyes front.

3

Line 11:

Right hand passing across chest on line with shoulder and pointing directly to left, eyes and head toward left.

"A cry of defiance, and not of fear!"

4

Lines 12 and 13:

On first line head turning again to front, on second line hands crossing one above the other in front of waist, then to lateral, palms supine.

5

Line 14:

Pos. 6. Transition—hands again to front, the right crossing above left, then passing into upper zone at full arm's length above head, palm facing front, left hand at same time passing into lower zone, near side, palm prone.

6

Lines 15 and 16:

Transition—right hand passing front, shoulder-high, then in to forehead on "Good-night," and outward and downward to side.

7

Line 17:

Pos. 5. Left hand rising on line with shoulder, lateral, palm prone, face toward left.

8

Lines 18 and 19:

Left hand moving inward toward chest, then outward again to same position, finger tips slightly upward.

9

Lines 20 and 21:

On first part of first line right hand carried over to left side, in same direction as left hand, palms of both vertical, body retreated somewhat to right; on remainder of lines retain same attitude, except that hands are carried higher.

10

Lines 22 and 23:

Retain preceding attitude, except that hands are lower and body inclined toward left.

11

Lines 24, 25, 26, 27, 28, and 29:

Pos. 2. Right knee bent, head forward. Transition —hands carried to upper zone, then outward and downward into middle zone, then the right, near ear as if listening, the left to lower zone, lateral, palm prone, eyes wandering

12

Line 30:

Position centred. Transition—hands rising upward, then slowly descending to side, eyes front.

13

Lines 31, 32, and 33:

Pos. 3. Transition—right hand to upper zone, oblique

front, finger tips upward, palm facing front, left to lower zone, oblique back, palm prone, eyes in same direction as right hand.

14

Lines 34, 35, and 36:

Line of gravity shifted to left foot. Transition—hands to upper zone front, then outward to lateral, palms vertical on "Startled," then hands curving inward front and out again to lateral on "Round," same repetition on "Masses" and on "Shapes of shade," making three distinct circles, then descending to lower zone, lateral.

15

Lines 37 and 38:

Line of gravity to right foot. Transition—hands to lower zone, front, then right hand passing high into upper zone, oblique front, index finger leading, left hand to lower zone near side.

16

Lines 39, 40, and 41:

Body well forward and eyes looking downward, right forearm carried directly before and within a few inches of forehead, palm of hand facing front.

17

Lines 42, 43, and 44:

Transition—both hands from upper zone downward and inward to middle zone, front, palms prone.

18

Lines 45, 46, 47, and 48:

Transition—both hands pass from front over toward left, then toward right, then to front, on "Seeming," then separating and moving to lateral and down to side.

19

Lines 49, 50, and 51:

Pos. 6. (Narrow)—head slightly drawn in to shoulders, one hand enclosing the other as if in dread, eyes moving.

20

Lines 52 and 53:

Pos. 1. Head and eyes in same direction as body, whole manner alive, hands to middle zone, oblique front, palms vertical.

21

Line 54:

Transition—hands moving in toward chest, crossing one above the other, then outward again as in preceding attitude, except somewhat broader.

22

Lines 55 and 56:

Transition—hands move in toward each other, then make three or four undulating movements outward, and float slowly down to side.

23

Lines 57, 58, and 59:
Pos. 7.   Face front.

24

Line 60:
Bring hands upward from side, to middle zone, oblique—front, right, left hand supine, right hand prone with gentle motion as if caressing.

25

Line 61:
Body thrown a little forward to oblique—right, eyes looking distantly in same direction, right hand over brows as if shielding eyes, left hand down and out at side, palm prone, whole manner interested.

26

Lines 62 and 63:
Pos. centred. Stamp right foot strongly on word " stamped," at same time quickly bring hands in fists from upper zone, front, down close to side.

27

Lines 64, 65, 66, and 67:
Pos. 3—but line of gravity in left foot, arms folded, head somewhat raised, eyes looking to oblique—right and upward.

28

Line 68:
Arms unfold, and carry hands to upper zone, oblique —front, right, palms vertical.

29

Line 69:

Hands in same position as preceding, with tremulous movement on "Glimmer," and quick upward motion on "Gleam."

30

Line 70:

Pos. 8—Quickly, with whole body turned away from front, hands in fists brought by straight-line arm movement, in front of and near waist, left hand a little lower than right.

31

Line 71:

Attitude same as preceding, except looking outward and upward over right shoulder.

32

Line 72:

Pos. 3—Quickly—right hand direct to upper zone, oblique front, right, index finger strong, left at same time to lower zone, lateral, palm prone.

33

Lines 73, 74, and 75:

Transition—hands to middle zone front, palms prone, eyes looking front, whole manner animated.

34

Line 76:

Hands passing with energy by straight-line arm

movement to lower zone lateral, index fingers strong on " Struck out."

35

Lines 77 and 78:

Transition—hands to middle zone front, palms supine on "That was all," then right hand to upper zone, palm vertical, left at same time to lower zone lateral, palm prone.

36

Lines 79 and 80:

Transition—hands passing to middle zone, front, one crossing above the other, then to oblique front, palms supine.

Omit lines 81, 82, 83, 84, 85, and 86.

37

Lines 87 and 88:

Line of gravity to left foot, and base narrowed. Transition—right hand passing to middle zone, front, palm supine, left at same time down at side.

38

Lines 89, 90, 91, and 92:

Transition—hands to lower zone front, and clasped near body for first two lines, then still clasped, to middle zone front, with shoulders shrugged, eyes and ears as if listening; hands passing outward and descending to side at close of lines.

39

Lines 93, 94, 95, and 96:

Transition—left hand to upper zone, oblique front, palm vertical, on "Gilded weathercock," then inward toward front, and out again to oblique front on next line, eyes in same direction.

40

Lines 97, 98, 99, and 100:

Pos. 4. Body somewhat retreated. Transition—right hand passing high into middle zone, front, and left into upper zone, oblique front, left, palms of both vertical, then both outward and down to side on last line.

41

Lines 101 and 102:

Pos. 5. (Narrow.) Right hand passing to middle zone, front, palm supine.

42

Lines 103 and 104.

Transition—both hands into upper zone, oblique front, palms vertical, finger tips more strongly upward on second line.

43

Lines 105 and 106:

Transition—hands downward and inward to middle zone, then outward to oblique front, palms prone, and downward to side on last line.

44

Lines 107 and 108:

Transition—right hand to middle zone, front, palm supine on " One."

45

Lines 109 and 110:

Transition—left hand to middle zone, front, then both hands rising and then passing downward into lower zone, front, palms prone, face and eyes downward.

46

Lines 111 and 112:

Transition—hands to middle zone, front, palms supine on first line, then quickly into upper zone, palms vertical on " Fired," then both directly to left on " Fled."

47

Lines 113 and 114:

Transition—hands to right oblique, forward, palms supine, eyes following.

48

Line 115:

Line of gravity to left foot. Transition—hands to left, palms vertical, eyes following.

49

Lines 116, 117, and 118:

Transition—hands curving inward toward front of

chest and crossing one above the other, palms outward, then slowly floating down to side, face front.

50

Lines 119, 120, and 121:
Line of gravity to right foot on first word and position retained.

51

Line 122:
Pos. 6. Transition—left hand in fist at right shoulder, left elbow high and on line with chin, right hand in fist, lower zone, oblique back, and well extended, whole expression firm.

52

Line 123:
Pos. 5. Transition—right hand to middle zone, oblique front and moved as if in the act of knocking, on the words " A knock at the door," left at same time to lower zone, lateral, palm prone.

53

Line 124:
Transition—right hand to lateral, palm supine.

54

Line 125:
Pos. 4. Transition—right hand to oblique back, palm supine.

55

Lines 126 and 127:

Pos. 5. Transition—both hands to middle zone, front, palms supine.

56

Line 128:

Transition—hands a little above middle zone, palms vertical, eyes raised oblique front, right.

57

Lines 129 and 130:

Transition—hands moving in toward head then outward and slowly dropping to side, face front.

THE FAMINE

FROM " HIAWATHA," LONGFELLOW

THE PANTOMIME

ATTITUDE

1

Lines 1 and 2:
Position 6. (Narrow.) Arms hanging downward in front of body, hands clasped, eyes looking front.

2

Lines 3 and 4:
Transition—hands passing upward front, to height of shoulder, then to oblique front, palms prone, descending and moving outward a little more on each repetition of "Thicker."

3

Lines 5 and 6:
Transition—as before, only somewhat higher, both hands descending well into lower zone, and each then slightly rising on each repetition of "Deeper,"—hold position through second line.

4

Line 7:
Transition—same as before but still higher, then descending into middle zone, lateral.

"With both hands his face he covered;
Seven long days and nights he sat there!"

5

Line 8:

Pos. 7. Transition—hands passing to middle zone, front, then right hand to lateral, palm supine, on " Through the forest," left floating down to side, then left hand to front, middle zone and out to lateral, palm vertical and right hand descending to side, on remainder of line, eyes in each case following.

6

Lines 9 and 10:

Pos. 5. Transition—hands near chest, palms vertical, finger tips upward, then thrust forward in middle zone, front on " Force."

7

Line 11:

Transition—hands curving inward, then front, palms supine on first part, repeated with hands lower on second part.

8

Line 12:

Line of gravity to left foot. Hands enclosing each other, at arm's length behind back and close to body.

9

Line 13:

Look upward and around on first part of line, and downward and around on second part of line.

10

Lines 14 and 15:

Transitions—for first line, right hand curved inward toward left chest, then to lower zone, oblique front, index finger leading. On second line repeat same arm movement, hand position prone.

11

Lines 16 and 17:

Transition—hands carried to upper zone front, then outward and downward, descending to side as if lifeless.

12

Line 18:

Transition—hands crossing middle zone, front, then carried to lower zone, front, palms supine.

Omit lines 19, 20, 21, 22, 23, 24, 25, 26, 27, and 28.

13

Lines 29, 30, and 31:

Pos. 2. Transition—hands over head, then downward into middle zone, front, palms vertical, eyes looking in same direction.

14

Lines 32 and 33:

Transition—hands moving toward oblique front, left, eyes following.

15

Lines 34 and 35:
Hands held strongly in same position.

16

Lines 36 and 37:
Hands raised somewhat higher, body slightly more retreated, face strongly expressive.

17

Lines 38 and 39:
Pos. 3. With stealthy movement. Transition—hands moving inward toward chest, then returning to former position, fingers crooked and spread, appearance weak and trembling, face haggard.

18

Lines 40 and 41:
Line of gravity to left foot. Transition—hands in toward chest, then high above head, fingers somewhat separated, palms vertical, whole manner aggressive, eyes looking downward and forward, oblique front, right.

19

Lines 42, 43, and 44:
Same attitude as preceding, except hands pass slowly outward and downward into lower zone front.

20

Lines 45, 46, and 47:
Pos. 8. Transition—hands from lower zone front,

upward and outward, then inward on face, covering temples with palms and forefingers, head drooped.

21

Lines 48 and 49:

Transition—hands rising from face, palms upward, head turned oblique, front, right, eyes looking forward and upward, expression terrified.

22

Lines 50 and 51:

Pos 1. Body strongly forward. Transition—hands downward into lower zone, then upward and inward toward chest and forward, by straight-line movement, palms prone, left hand slightly in advance of right.

23

Lines 52, 53, 54, and 55:

Transition—hands to upper zone, front, then outward and downward, the right passing inward and placed on heart, the left at same time descending near side and clinched, face sad but firm. On third line the left rises and is placed with palm strongly on forehead, head slightly thrown back, eyes looking forward and somewhat upward.

24

Lines 56 and 57:

Pos. centred. Transition—(through first line) hands to upper zone, then descending; then on second line right hand passing over toward left shoulder, then again to upper zone, right, and at full arm's length directly above head, index finger pointing upward, left hand at right shoulder, index finger pointing to right arm, eyes looking upward at right hand, as if estimating length of bow.

25

Line 58:

Attitude same as preceding, except that right hand descends and passes to left shoulder, index finger pointing backward, eyes front.

26

Lines 59, 60, and 61:

Transition—hands passing to upper zone, then downward to middle zone, front, palms supine.

27

Lines 62, 63, 64, 65, and 66:

Pos. 5. Transition—hands quickly to upper zone, front, then outward and downward, and inward in middle zone, and applied palm to palm near chest, finger tips upward, elbows outward, head and eyes raised, whole manner fervent.

28

Lines 67, 68, 69, 70, 71, 72, 73, 74, and 75:

With interlocked fingers, bring hands close to chest, elbows high, whole manner intense, retain attitude to end of lines.

Omit lines 76 to 88 inclusive.

29

Lines 89, 90, 91, 92, and 93:

Pos. 3. Transition—hands to upper zone, front, then outward and downward, and inward in lower zone, then forward to oblique front, right, palms prone, face in same direction, countenance sad, eyes looking forward and downward.

30

Lines 94, 95, 96, and 97:

Line of gravity to left foot, body inclining to left side, left hand near left ear as if listening, right hand down and out at right side, palm prone, eyes looking forward and upward, oblique front, right.

31

Lines 98 and 99:

Line of gravity to right foot, body inclined forward and slightly downward. Transition—hands to upper zone, then through oblique front to lower zone, then inward and forward to oblique front, right, palms prone, face sympathetic, eyes looking downward.

32

Lines 100, 101, 102, and 103:

Pos. 7. Transition—hands to upper zone, then left hand outward and downward to left side, palm prone, right hand at same time passing to right lateral, index finger leading, hand position a little above shoulder; on third line slightly beckon twice with right hand, eyes looking distantly forward to right, face wistful and sad.

33

Lines 104 and 105:

Attitude same as in No. 31, except somewhat stronger and more sympathetic.

34

Lines 106 and 107:

Pos. 2. Body strongly retreated. Transition—hands to upper zone front, then outward and inward and upward, and held over head, fingers separated, palms vertical, elbows outward, whole manner terrified.

35

Lines 108 and 109:

Attitude same as preceding, except hands tightly close on beginning of second line.

36

Line 110:

Head thrown backward, hands clasping same as if in anguish, elbows upward and outward, face indicative of death.

37

Lines 111, 112, 113, 114, 115, 116, and 117:

Pos. 5. Transition—hands to upper zone, front, then downward and inward, the right then passing to lower zone, lateral, palm prone, the left in toward chest, then to oblique front, left, index finger leading, eyes looking in same direction.

38

Lines 118, 119, and 120:

Pos. 6. Transition—hands crossing one above the other in middle zone front, then outward and downward into lower zone, oblique front, palms prone, on first line, then to upper zone, oblique front, on second line, palms vertical and held to end of lines, eyes looking upward.

39

Line 121:
Hands dropped to side, head and eyes downward.

40

Lines 122, 123, and 124:
Body and head inclined slightly to right, right hand carried toward right ear as if listening, left in lower zone, out at side, palm prone, eyes raised oblique front, left, face sad and anxious.

Omit lines 125 and 126.

41

Line 127:
Pos. 3. Body strongly forward. Transition—hands to middle zone, front, near waist, then with straight line movement to oblique front, right, palms supine, eyes looking in same direction, expression eager and anxious.

Omit lines 128 and 129.

42

Lines 130 and 131:

Pos. 2. Knees bent, hands thrown above head, arms slightly relaxed at elbows, palms vertical, face oblique front, right, and expressive of anguish.

43

Lines 132 and 133:

Transition—hands outward and descending into middle zone, then inward and placed one upon the other in the region of the heart.

44

Lines 134, 135, and 136:

Knees firm. Transition—hands passing to upper zone, oblique front, palms supine, on first line, then carried inward, palms vertical on "Stars," then outward to oblique front on "Shook" and held to end of line.

45

Lines 137, 138, 139, 140, 141, 142, 143, 144, 145, 146, 147, 148, and 149:

Retain pos. 2 and kneel to floor on right knee. Movement very slow and dejected, face buried in palms, with hands resting on left knee.

Omit 150 to 155 inclusive.

46

Lines 156, 157, 158, 159, 160, 161, and 162:

Retain preceding attitude for first four lines, then

turn palms of hands down, one upon the other upon left knee, at same time slowly bringing up head and body without raising right knee from floor, shoulders drooped, face sad, eyes looking obliquely forward, right.

47

Lines 163, 164, 165, 166, and 167:
Retaining hands on knee rise slowly to position 3, line of gravity in left foot: having risen, tightly clasp hands at arm's length in lower zone and close to body, face and eyes oblique front, right, whole manner mournful.

48

Lines 168 and 169:
Line of gravity very slowly to right foot, left hand at same time passing to lower zone, lateral, palm prone, right hand in toward left shoulder, then well forward to oblique front, right, palm supine, eyes looking distantly in same direction.

49

Lines 170, 171, 172, 173, 174, 175, and 176:
Transition—hands slowly moving inward and placed upon heart, elbows well out, retain this attitude to end of lines.

50

Lines 177 and 178:
Transition—right hand slowly passing outward to oblique front, right, palm supine, face wistful.

51

Line 179:

Line of gravity to left foot, right hand at same time passing upward and inward until almost directly overhead, index finger leading, eyes looking upward in direction indicated by finger.

52

Line 180:

Transition—left hand passing from heart to upper zone front, then both passing outward and downward, then inward toward chest, then to upper zone oblique front, palms supine, and held to close, head and eyes raised.

THE BACHELOR'S SALE

I dreamed a dream, in the midst of my slumbers,
And as fast as I dreamed it was coined into numbers;
My thoughts ran along in such beautiful meter
I'm sure I ne'er saw any poetry sweeter.

It seemed that a law had been recently made,
That a tax on old bachelors' pates should be laid,
And, in order to make them all willing to marry,
The tax was as large as a man could well carry.

The bachelors grumbled and said 'twas " no use,"
'Twas " cruel injustice " and " horrid abuse;"
And declared that to keep their own heart's blood from
    spilling
Of such a vile tax they would pay ne'er a shilling.

But the rulers determined their scheme to pursue,
Set all the old bachelors up at vendu,
And a crier was sent through the town, to and fro,
To rattle his bell and his trumpet to blow.

And to call out to all he might meet on the way
" Ho! forty old bachelors for sale here to-day."
And presently all the old maids in the town,
Each one in her very best bonnet and gown,

"Each lugged an old bachelor home on her shoulder."

From thirty to sixty, fair, plump, red, and pale,
Of every description all flocked to the sale.

The auctioneer then in his labors began,
And called out aloud as they held up a man,
" How much for this bachelor? who wants to buy?"
In a twink every maiden responded " I," " I."

In short, at a hugely extravagant price,
The bachelors were all sold off in a trice;
And forty maidens, some younger, some older,
Each lugged an old bachelor home on her shoulder.

THE BACHELOR'S SALE

ATTITUDE

1

"I dreamed a dream, in the midst of my slumbers,
And as fast as I dreamed it was coined into numbers;
My thoughts ran along in such beautiful meter
I'm sure I ne'er saw any poetry sweeter."

Pos. 3. (Narrow.) Line of gravity in left foot, fingers loosely interlocked in lower zone, front and close to body, eyes looking forward, amused expression.

2

"It seemed that a law had been recently made,
That a tax on old bachelors' pates should be laid,"

Transition—right hand in toward left chest, then to middle zone, front, palm supine on "Law," left passing down to side; on second line right hand passes inward again to left, then forward to same position as before on "Pates," except that palm should be prone.

3

"And, in order to make them all willing to marry,
The tax was as large as a man could well carry."

Transition—hands crossing one above the other in middle zone, front, then passing outward to oblique front, palms supine.

4

"The bachelors grumbled and said 'twas 'no use,'
'Twas 'cruel injustice' and 'horrid abuse;'"

Hands behind back, whole manner decided, head in very emphatic nod on "Cruel injustice," and also on "horrid abuse."

5

"And declared that to keep their own heart's blood from spilling
Of such a vile tax they would pay ne'er a shilling."

Body drawn up firmly, right hand raised decidedly, high over head on first line, then brought in fist into lower zone, front, on "Vile tax" and held to end of stanza, expression very firm.

6

"But the rulers determined their scheme to pursue,
Set all the bachelors up at vendu,"

Transition—hands passing to middle zone front, one crossing above the other, then to oblique front, palms supine.

7

"And a crier was sent through the town, to and fro,
To rattle his bell and his trumpet to blow."

Transition—on first line hands move inward and cross one above the other and outward toward lateral, the left then passing down near side and the right moved strongly toward left, then toward right and held on "To rattle his bell."

8

"And to call out to all he might meet on the way"

Transition—hands inward to middle zone, front, then to oblique front, palms supine.

9

"'Ho! forty old bachelors for sale here to-day.'"

Transition—right hand to mouth as if shouting, left hand on left hip, head slightly raised and turned toward oblique front, left.

10

"And presently all the old maids of the town,
Each one in her very best bonnet and gown,
From thirty to sixty, fair, plump, red, and pale,
Of every description all flocked to the sale."

Retain preceding attitude on first three lines, then hands transition by middle zone, front, to oblique front, palms supine for last line, eyes front.

11

"The auctioneer then in his labors began,
And called out aloud as they held up a man,
'How much for this bachelor? who wants to buy?'"

Retain preceding attitude on first line, then to Pos. 4 on second line. Transition—hands moving into upper zone and downward to oblique front, left, palms supine, left hand higher than right, eyes also to oblique left.

12

"In a twink every maiden responded 'I,' 'I.'"

Pos. 3. Body inclined forward. Transition—hands passing into upper zone, then outward and downward, the right placed near mouth as if calling, and the left moving to lower zone, lateral, palm prone, eyes and face oblique forward to right, mouth open as if shouting.

13

"In short, at a hugely extravagant price,
The bachelors were all sold off in a trice;
And forty old maidens, some younger, some older,
Each lugged an old bachelor home on her shoulder."

Retain preceding attitude on first two lines; on third line, the line of gravity should be slowly shifted to left foot, the hands at same time passing to lower zone, front, then into upper zone, then outward and downward and in close upon left shoulder for last line, face turned oblique front, left, and somewhat raised, eyes toward oblique left backward, expression mirthful.

QUEEN VASHTI'S LAMENT

ABRIDGED

"And after these things, when the wrath of King Ahasuerus was appeased, he remembered Vashti and what she had done, and what was decreed against her."
—ESTHER ii, 1.

Is this all the love that he bore me, my husband, to
    publish my face
To the nobles of Media and Persia, whose hearts are
    besotted and base?
Did he think me a slave, me, Vashti, the Beautiful, me,
    Queen of queens,
To summon me thus for a show to the midst of his
    bacchanal scenes?

I stand like an image of brass, I, Vashti, in sight of
    such men!
No, sooner, a thousand times sooner, the mouth of the
    lioness' den.

Did he love me, or is he, too, though the King, but a
    brute like the rest!
I have seen him in wine, and I fancied 'twas then that
    he loved me the best;

"And the King shall love his Vashti; his Beautiful, his own."

But ever before, in his wine, toward me he showed
    honor and grace;
He was King, I was Queen, and those nobles, he made
    them remember their place,
But now all is changed; I am vile, they are honored,
    they push me aside,
A butt for Memucan and Shethar and Meres, gone mad
    in their pride!

Shall I faint, shall I pine, shall I sicken and die for the
    loss of his love?
Not I; I am queen of myself, though the stars fall
    from heaven above.
The stars! ha! the torment is there, for my light is put
    out by a star,
That has dazzled the eyes of the King and his court
    and his captains of war.

He was lonely, they say, and he looked like a ghost, as
    he sat at his wine,
On the couch, where, of yore, by his side, his Beautiful
    used to recline;
But the King is a slave to his pride, to his oath and the
    laws of the Medes,
And he cannot call Vashti again, though his poor heart
    is wounded and bleeds.

So they sought through the land for a wife, while the
    King thought of me all the while—
I can see him, this moment, with eyes that are lost for
    the loss of a smile,

Gazing dreamily on while each maiden is temptingly
    passed in review,
While the love in his heart is awake with the thought
    of a face that he knew!

Then she came, when his heart was grown weary with
    loving the dream of the past!
She is fair—I could curse her for that, if I thought that
    this passion would last!
But, e'en if it last, all the love is for me, and, through
    good and through ill,
The King will remember his Vashti, will think of his
    Beautiful still.

What is it? Oft as I lie awake and my pillow is wet
    with tears
There comes—it came to me just now—a flash, then
    disappears;
A flash of thought that makes this life a re-enacted
    scene,
That makes me dream what was will be, and what is
    now, has been

And I, when age on age has rolled, shall sit on the
    royal throne,
And the King shall love his Vashti, his Beautiful, his
    own,
And for the joy of what has been and what again will
    be,
I'll try to bear this awful weight of lonely misery!

The star! Queen Esther! blazing light that burns into
    my soul!
The star! the star! Oh! flickering light of life beyond
    control!
O King! remember Vashti, thy Beautiful, thy own,
Who loved thee and will love thee still, when Esther's
    light has flown!

JOHN READE.

THE PANTOMIME

ATTITUDE

1

"Is this all the love that he bore me, my husband, to publish my face
To the nobles of Media and Persia, whose hearts are besotted and base?
Did he think me a slave, me, Vasthi, the Beautiful, me, Queen of queens,
To summon me thus for a show to the midst of his bacchanal scenes?"

Pos. 6. Body well drawn up, arms folded, face oblique front, right, expression indignant, eyes a little above horizontal.

2

"I stand like an image of brass, I, Vashti, in sight of such men!"

Pos. 5. Transition—hands unfolding, rising to upper zone, front, then outward and downward to middle zone, oblique front, palms supine, face front.

3

"No, sooner, a thousand times sooner, the mouth of the lioness' den."

Pos. 6. Transition— hands carried quickly above head, then brought firmly down with straight-line arm movement, near side, hands closing in fists.

4

"Did he love me, or is he, too, though the King, but a brute like the rest!
I have seen him in wine, and I fancied 'twas then that he loved me the best;
But ever before, in his wine, toward me he showed honor and grace;"

Transition—hands clasped at arm's length, in lower zone, front, near body, head drooped; features relaxed, whole manner meditative.

5

"He was King, I was Queen,

Body and head well drawn up, eyes front. Transition—hands passing a little above middle zone, then right hand to middle zone, oblique front, palm supine, left hand downward to side, palm prone, right hand moved a little further outward and upward on "Queen."

6

"And those nobles, he made them remember their place,"

Transition—right hand passing to upper zone, then to lower zone, lateral, straight-line arm movement, palm prone.

7

"But now all is changed;"

A slight shrug of shoulders, as if showing contempt, facial expression to correspond.

8

"I am vile, they are honored,"

Transition—hands to front of waist, crossing one above the other and returning to lower zone, lateral, palms facing front, head lowered as if in mock humility.

9

"They push me aside,
A butt for Memucan and Shethar and Meres, gone mad in their pride!"

Pos. 7. Transition—right hand passing over to left side, then both hands passing directly to right side, middle zone, palms vertical (right hand furthest extended) on "push me aside," and held, face oblique forward left.

10

"Shall I faint, shall I pine, shall I sicken and die for the loss of his love?"

Line of gravity to left foot. Transition—hands to upper zone front, then outward and downward at side.

11

"Not I; I am queen of myself,"

Body drawn strongly up, right hand passing upward to middle zone, then brought inward with fingers touching chest on "queen of myself."

12

"Though the stars fall from heaven above."

Transition—right hand carried quickly at arm's length above head, palm facing front, whole manner firm, eyes raised.

13

"The stars! ha! the torment is there, for my light is put out by a star,
That has dazzled the eyes of the King and his court and his captains of war."

Right hand clasping back of head just above neck, elbow well up and oblique forward, left hand well out at side and clinched, head drooped.

14

"He was lonely, they say, and he looked like a ghost as he sat at his wine,
On the couch, where, of yore, by his side, his Beautiful used to recline;"

Transition—right hand passing outward and downward to lower zone front, left hand to same position from lower zone, then one inclosing the other near body, muscles relaxed, manner meditative.

15

"But the King is a slave to his pride, to his oath and the laws of the Medes,"

Head slowly rising.

16

"And he cannot call Vasthti again, though his poor heart is wounded and bleeds."

Hands brought slowly upward, clasped and placed upon chest, eyes slightly raised, face sad and sympathetic.

17

"So they sought through the land for a wife, while the King thought of me all the while—"

Hands loosely clasped, dropping again into lower zone near body.

18

"I can see him, this moment, with eyes that are lost for the loss of a smile,
Gazing dreamily on while each maiden is temptingly passed in review,"

Pos. 5. (Narrow.) Eyes obliquely forward, right, face sad.

19

"While the love in his heart is awake with the thought of a face that he knew!"

Transition—hands passing upward to middle zone, front, palms supine.

20

"Then she came, when his heart was grown weary with loving the dream of the past!"

Line of gravity to left foot. Transition—hands passing to upper zone, front then outward and downward at side.

21

"She is fair—I could curse her for that, if I thought that this passion would last!"

Line of gravity to right foot. Transition—hands quickly passing to front of chest, then by straight-line arm movement to lower zone, lateral, close to side, palms prone, whole manner strong.

22

"But, e'en if it last, all the love is for me, and through good and through ill,
The King will remember his Vashti, will think of his Beautiful still."

Transition—hands moving slowly front, in lower zone, fingers loosely interlocking, face obliquely forward to right, eyes a little above middle range, expression sadly meditative.

23

"What is it? Oft as I lie awake and my pillow is wet
  with tears
There comes—it came to me just now—a flash, then
  disappears;"

Line of gravity to left foot. Face (on first line) obliquely forward, left, then slowly toward front on second line, eyes still a little above middle range. Transition—hands rising to height of head on "There comes," then inward, finger tips touching head, then outward on "Disappears."

24

"A flash of thought that makes this life a re-enacted
  scene,
That makes me dream what was, will be, and what is
  now, has been.
And I, when age on age has rolled, shall sit on the royal
  throne,
And the King shall love his Vashti, his Beautiful, his
  own,"

Line of gravity to left foot. Transition—hands passing downward from "Disappears" into lower zone, front, then applied palm to palm, and brought to left side of neck, elbows well out and up, head resting against back of right hand and thrown slightly back, eyes looking somewhat upward and forward toward oblique front, left, face sadly reflective but hopeful.

25

" And for the joy of what has been and what again will be,
I'll try to bear this awful weight of lonely misery!"

Transition—hands slowly unclasping and passing to upper zone, on first line, then outward to lower zone, lateral, on second line, palms prone, face front, head drooped.

26

"The star! Queen Esther! blazing light that burns into my soul!
The star! the star! Oh! flickering light of life beyond control!"

Transition—hands passing to upper zone, front, then right hand brought, in fist, strongly upon chest, left in fist, to lower zone, lateral, and well extended, whole manner strong, head and eyes raised.

27

"O King! remember Vashti, thy Beautiful, thy own,
Who loved thee and will love thee still, when Esther's light has flown!"

Pos. 3. (Narrow.) Transition—hands passing to upper zone, front, then outward and downward, to middle zone, oblique front, palms supine, face oblique forward, right, expression yearning, hands clasped in front of chest on last line.

THE VOICE OF SPRING

I come, I come! ye have called me long—
I come o'er the mountains with light and song!
Ye may trace my step o'er the wakening earth,
By the winds which tell of the violet's birth,
By the primrose-stars in the shadowy grass,
By the green leaves opening as I pass.

I have breathed on the South, and the chestnut flowers
By thousands have burst from the forest-bowers,
And the ancient graves and the fallen fanes
Are veiled with wreaths on Italian plains;—
But it is not for me, in my hour of bloom,
To speak of the ruin or the tomb!

I have looked on the hills of the stormy North,
And the larch has hung all his tassels forth,
And the fisher is out on the sunny sea,
And the reindeer bounds o'er the pastures free,
And the pine has a fringe of softer green,
And the moss looks bright where my foot hath been.

I have sent through the wood-paths a glowing sigh,
And called out each voice of the deep blue sky;
From the night-bird's lay through the starry time,
In the groves of the soft Hesperian clime,

"I shall find them there with their eyes of light!"

To the swan's wild note by the Iceland lakes,
When the dark fir-branch into verdure breaks.

From the streams and founts I have loosed the chain,
They are sweeping on to the silvery main,
They are flashing down from the mountain brows,
They are flinging spray o'er the forest boughs,
They are bursting fresh from their sparry caves,
And the earth resounds with the joy of waves!

Come forth, O ye children of gladness! come!
Where the violets lie may be now your home.
Ye of the rose-lip and dew-bright eye,
And the bounding footstep to meet me fly!
With the lyre, and the wreath, and the joyous lay,
Come forth to the sunshine—I may not stay.

Away from the dwellings of care-worn men,
The waters are sparkling in grove and glen!
Away from the chamber and sullen hearth,
The young leaves are dancing in breezy mirth!
Their light stems thrill to the wild-wood strains,
And youth is abroad in my green domains.

But ye!—ye are changed since ye met me last!
There is something bright from your features passed!
There is that come over your brow and eye
Which speaks of a world where the flowers must die!
—Ye smile! but your smile hath a dimness yet.
Oh! what have ye looked on since last we met?

Ye are changed, ye are changed—and I see not here
All whom I saw in the vanished year!
There were graceful heads, with their ringlets bright,
Which tossed in the breeze with a play of light;
They were eyes in whose glistening laughter lay
No faint remembrance of dull decay!

There were steps that flew o'er the cowslip's head,
As if for a banquet all earth were spread;
There were voices that rang through the sapphire sky,
And had not a sound of mortality!
Are they gone? is their mirth from the mountains
    passed?—
Ye have looked on death since ye met me last!

I know whence the shadow comes o'er you now—
Ye have strewn the dust on the sunny brow!
Ye have given the lovely to earth's embrace—
She hath taken the fairest of beauty's race,
With their laughing eyes and their festal crown;
They are gone from amongst you in silence down!

They are gone from amongst you, the young and fair,
Ye have lost the gleam of their shining hair!
But I know of a land where there falls no blight—
I shall find them there, with their eyes of light!
Where Death midst the blooms of the morn may dwell,
I tarry no longer—farewell, farewell!

THE PANTOMIME

The dress for this Pantomime will be improved if decorated with sprays or wreaths of flowers.

ATTITUDE

1

" I come, I come! ye have called me long—"

Pos. 2. Hands high over head, finger tips touching, palm of left supine, palm of right prone, face bright, body well drawn up, movements light and airy.

2

"I come o'er the mountains with light and song!"

Pos. 5. Hands quickly brought outward and downward into lower zone, front, then into upper zone as in first attitude, except hand position is reversed.

3

" Ye may trace my steps o'er the wakening earth,
By the winds which tell of the violet's birth,
By the primrose-stars in the shadowy grass,
By the green leaves opening as I pass."

Hand transition outward and downward lateral, then short curves inward and outward, shoulder high on

"By the winds," then downward into lower zone on "Violet's birth," then inward and outward, palms prone, on "Primrose-stars," then upward into middle realm and inward and outward on "Green leaves."

4

"I have breathed on the South, and the chestnut flowers
  By thousands have burst from the forest-bowers,
  And the ancient graves and the fallen fanes,
  Are veiled with wreaths on Italian plains;—"

Pos. 8. Hand transition to lower zone front and crossing one above the other and outward to oblique front, upper zone, palms vertical on "Thousands" and held to end of next line, when they descend into middle zone on "Veiled," palm prone.

5

"But it is not for me, in my hour of bloom,
  To speak of the ruin or the tomb!"

Pos. 5—(Narrow.) Line of gravity in left foot. Transition—hands descending into lower zone front, fingers loosely clasped, face looking front.

6

"I have looked on the hills of the stormy North,"

Pos. 3. Transition—both hands rising into upper zone, front, then curving outward and downward and inward toward chest, then right hand forward and slightly into upper zone, oblique front, palm nearly prone, left at same time descending to lower zone oblique back, palm prone.

7

"And the larch has hung all his tassels forth,"

Right hand rising slowly and well into upper zone and somewhat dropped at wrist.

8

"The fisher is out on the sunny sea,"

Body inclined a little more directly to right. Transition—hands passing in toward chest, then curving outward and obliquely forward to right, right hand considerably in advance of left, palms vertical.

9

"And the reindeer bounds o'er the pastures free,"

Line of gravity shifted to left foot, body more drawn up, right hand a little distance in front but above head, left a few inches from chest, palms facing front, elbows well out, face looking forward.

10

"And the pine has a fringe of softer green,"

Same as preceding, except face is looking upward.

11

"And the moss looks bright, where my foot hath been."

Hands and head slowly descending.

12

"I have sent through the wood-paths a glowing sigh,"

Pos. 7. Transition—hands passing from lower zone, lateral, to middle zone, front, right crossing above left, then passing to lateral—left at same time to lower zone near side, palm slightly prone.

13

"And called out each voice of the deep blue sky;"

Right hand passing in toward left chest, then high into upper zone, right side, palm partly facing front, eyes looking up.

14

"From the night-bird's lay through the starry time,
In the groves of the soft Hesperian clime,"

Right hand passing gently inward in upper zone, then oblique back, right, palm well up, eyes looking direction of right hand.

15

"To the swan's wild note by the Iceland lakes,"

Pos. 3. Hand transition by lower zone, front, right crossing above left, then passing to upper zone, oblique front, palm vertical, left at same time downward and out at side, palm prone.

16

"When the dark fir-branch into verdure breaks."

Right hand slowly rising higher, palm upward on "Breaks."

17

"From the streams and founts I have loosed the chain,"

Line of gravity to left foot. Transition—hands crossing in front of chest, then out and to lower zone oblique front, palms prone.

18

"They are sweeping on to the silvery main,"

Pos. 7. Transition—hands carried first to left side, lower zone, left hand most extended, then both swept to right side, lower zone, right hand most extended, palms prone.

19

"They are flashing down from the mountain brows;"

Hands swept to left oblique front, upper zone, left hand leading, palms upward.

20

"They are flinging spray o'er the forest boughs;"

Line of gravity to left foot. Transition—hands quickly carried inward toward forehead, then outward and upward to oblique front, palms vertical.

21

"They are bursting fresh from their sparry caves;"

Transition—hands downward and inward toward chest, then outward to oblique front, palms vertical.

22

"And the earth resounds with the joy of waves!"

Hands slowly descending to side.

23

"Come forth, O ye children of gladness! come!
Where the violets lie may be now your home.
Ye of the rose-lip and dew-bright eye,
And the bounding footstep to meet me fly!
With the lyre, and the wreath, and the joyous lay,
Come forth to the sunshine—I may not stay."

Pos. 5. Transition—hands to middle zone, oblique front and held, palms supine; on "Come forth to the sunshine" hands should move inward, then out to same position, eyes looking front.

24

"Away from the dwellings of care-worn men,
The waters are sparkling in grove and glen!
Away from the chamber and sullen hearth,
The young leaves are dancing in breezy mirth!
Their light stems thrill to the wild-wood strains,
And youth is abroad in my green domains."

Pos. 6. Transition—hands crossing front, then right hand passing to oblique right, back, middle zone, palm supine, left at same time descending to lower zone near side, palm prone.

25

"But ye!—ye are changed since ye met me last!
There is something bright from your features passed!
There is that come over your brow and eye
Which speaks of a world where the flowers must die!
—Ye smile! but your smile hath a dimness yet."

Transition—hands slowly descending into lower zone, front and held, fingers loosely interlocked, face looking front.

26

"Oh! what have ye looked on since last we met?"

Pos. 5. Transition—hands outward in lower zone, then inward near chest, one crossing above the other, then outward to oblique front, palms supine.

27

"Ye are changed, ye are changed—and I see not here
All whom I saw in the vanished year!"

Hand movement inward, then outward and retained, palms vertical.

28

"There were graceful heads, with their ringlets bright,
Which tossed in the breeze with a play of light;"

Transition—hands pass inward, then right hand outward to oblique front, palm supine, left at same time descending to lower zone near side, palm prone.

29

"There were eyes in whose glistening laughter lay
  No faint remembrance of dull decay!"

Right hand gently moved inward, then outward to previous position.

30

"There were steps that flew o'er the cowslip's head,"

Line of gravity to left foot. Transition—hands pass inward toward chest, then outward and downward into lower zone, oblique front, palms prone.

31

"As if for a banquet all earth were spread;"

Transition—hands move inward, then outward to lateral, palms supine.

32

"There were voices that rang through the sapphire sky,
  And had not a sound of mortality!"

Transition—right hand passes inward toward left chest, then into upper zone front, palm slightly upward, left hand down near side, palm prone.

33

"Are they gone? is their mirth from the mountains
  passed?"

Hands slowly descending to side.

34

" Ye have looked on death since ye met me last!"
" I know whence the shadow comes o'er you now—"

Line of gravity to right foot. Transition—hands outward in lower zone, then upward to front of chest and clasped, elbows well out, face sympathetic.

35

" Ye have strewn the dust on the sunny brow!"

Transition—hands pass into upper zone, then outward and downward to oblique front, lower zone, palms prone, eyes looking downward.

36

" Ye have given the lovely to earth's embrace—
  She hath taken the fairest of beauty's race,
  With their laughing eyes and their festal crown;"

Transition—hands pass inward, then outward to oblique front, palms front, finger-tips downward.

37

" They are gone from amongst you in silence down!
  They are gone from amongst you, the young and fair,
  Ye have lost the gleam of their shining hair!"

Transition—right hand rising toward left chest, then downward to oblique front, lower zone, left at same time by shorter curve to same zone near side, palms prone.

38

"But I know of a land where there falls no blight—"

Transition—right hand toward left chest, then to direct front, palm supine, face looking front.

39

"I shall find them there, with their eyes of light!"

Line of gravity to left foot, right hand pointing upward to fullest height, elbow and wrist straight, face looking upward.

40

"Where Death midst the blooms of the morn may dwell, I tarry no longer—"

Hand slowly descending to side.

41

"Farewell, farewell!"

Transition—hands carried into upper zone and waved upon each word as if bidding adieu, at same time body retreated by taking two or three steps backward.

"On this home by Horror haunted!"

THE RAVEN

ABRIDGED

Once upon a midnight dreary, while I ponder'd, weak and weary,
Over many a quaint and curious volume of forgotten lore,—
While I nodded, nearly napping, suddenly there came a tapping,
As of some one gently rapping, rapping at my chamber-door.
"'Tis some visitor," I muttered, "tapping at my chamber-door—
    Only this, and nothing more."

Ah, distinctly I remember, it was in the bleak December,
And each separate dying ember wrought its ghost upon the floor.
Eagerly I wish'd the morrow: vainly I had sought to borrow
From my books surcease of sorrow—sorrow for the lost Lenore—
For the rare and radiant maiden whom the angels name Lenore—
    Nameless here forevermore.

And the silken, sad, uncertain rustling of each purple
    curtain,
Thrill'd me—filled me with fantastic terrors never felt
    before;
So that now, to still the beating of my heart, I stood
    repeating,
" 'Tis some visitor entreating entrance at my chamber-
    door,—
Some late visitor entreating entrance at my chamber-
    door;
        That it is, and nothing more."

Presently my soul grew stronger: hesitating then no
    longer,
"Sir," said I, "or Madam, truly your forgiveness I
    implore;
But the fact is, I was napping, and so gently you came
    rapping,
And so faintly you came tapping, tapping at my chamber-
    door,
That I scarce was sure I heard you "—here I open'd wide
    the door:
        Darkness there, and nothing more.

Deep into that darkness peering, long I stood there,
    wondering, fearing,
Doubting, dreaming dreams no mortals ever dared to
    dream before;
But the silence was unbroken, and the stillness gave no
    token,

And the only word there spoken was the whisper'd word,
     "Lenore!"
This I whisper'd, and an echo murmur'd back the word,
     "LENORE!"
          Merely this, and nothing more.

Back into the chamber turning, all my soul within me
     burning,
Soon again I heard a tapping, something louder than
     before.
"Surely," said I, "surely that is something at my window-
     lattice;
Let me see then what thereat is, and this mystery
     explore,—
Let my heart be still a moment, and this mystery
     explore;—
          'Tis the wind, and nothing more."

Open here I flung the shutter, when with many a flirt
     and flutter,
In there stepp'd a stately raven of the saintly days of
     yore.
Not the least obeisance made he; not a minute stopp'd
     or stay'd he;
But, with mien of lord or lady, perch'd above my cham-
     ber-door,—
Perch'd upon a bust of Pallas, just above my chamber-
     door—
          Perched and sat and nothing more.

Then this ebony bird beguiling my sad fancy into smiling,
By the grave and stern decorum of the countenance it wore,
"Though thy crest be shorn and shaven, thou," I said, "art sure no craven;
Ghastly, grim, and ancient raven, wandering from the nightly shore,
Tell me what thy lordly name is on the Night's Plutonian shore?
      Quoth the raven, "Nevermore!"

Much I marvel'd this ungainly fowl to hear discourse so plainly,
Though its answer little meaning—little relevancy bore;
For we cannot help agreeing that no living human being
Ever yet was bless'd with seeing bird above his chamber-door—
Bird or beast upon the sculptured bust above his chamber-door,
      With such name as "Nevermore!"

But the raven still beguiling all my sad soul into smiling,
Straight I wheel'd a cushion'd seat in front of bird, and bust, and door.
Then, upon the velvet sinking, I betook myself to linking
Fancy unto fancy, thinking what this ominous bird of yore—

What this grim, ungainly, ghastly, gaunt, and ominous
  bird of yore
    Meant in croaking "Nevermore!"

This I sat engaged in guessing, but no syllable expressing
To the fowl, whose fiery eyes now burn'd into my bosom's
  core;
This and more I sat divining, with my head at ease
  reclining
On the cushion's velvet lining that the lamp-light
  gloated o'er,
But whose velvet violet lining, with the lamp-light gloating
  o'er,
    She shall press—ah! nevermore!

Then methought the air grew denser, perfumed from an
  unseen censer
Swung by seraphim, whose foot-falls tinkled on the
  tufted floor.
"Wretch," I cried, "thy God hath lent thee—by these
  angels he hath sent thee
Respite—respite and nepenthe from thy memories of
  Lenore!
Quaff, oh, quaff this kind nepenthe, and forget this lost
  Lenore!"
    Quoth the raven, "Nevermore!"

"Prophet!" said I, "thing of evil!—prophet still, if bird
  or devil!
Whether tempter sent, or whether tempest toss'd thee

Desolate, yet all undaunted, on this desert land enchanted—
On this home by Horror haunted—tell me truly, I implore—
Is there—is there balm in Gilead?—tell me—tell me, I implore!"
        Quoth the raven, "Nevermore!"

"Prophet!" said I, "thing of evil!—prophet still, if bird or devil!
By that heaven that bends above us—by that God we both adore,
Tell this soul, with sorrow laden, if, within the distant Aidenn,
It shall clasp a sainted maiden, whom the angels name Lenore;
Clasp a rare and radiant maiden, whom the angels name Lenore!"
        Quoth the raven, "Nevermore!"

"Be that word our sign of parting, bird or fiend!" I shriek'd, upstarting—
"Get thee back into the tempest and the Night's Plutonian shore!
Leave no black plume as a token of that lie thy soul hath spoken!
Leave my loneliness unbroken!—quit the bust above my door!
Take thy beak from out my heart, and take thy form from off my door!"

And the raven, never flitting, still is sitting, still is sitting
On the pallid bust of Pallas, just above my chamber-door;
And his eyes have all the seeming of a demon's that is dreaming,
And the lamp-light o'er him streaming throws his shadow on the floor;
And my soul from out that shadow that lies floating on the floor
    Shall be lifted—NEVERMORE!

                              EDGAR A. POE

THE PANTOMIME

ATTITUDE

1

"Once upon a midnight dreary, while I ponder'd, weak
    and weary,
Over many a quaint and curious volume of forgotten
    lore,—
While I nodded, nearly napping, suddenly there came
    a tapping,
As of some one gently rapping, rapping at my chamber-
    door.
"'Tis some visitor," I muttered, "tapping at my cham-
    ber-door—
    Only this, and nothing more."

Pos. 3—(narrow.) Line of gravity in left foot, left hand with fingers against left cheek, thumb under chin, right hand supporting elbow of left arm, head somewhat dropped; eyes looking downward; on "Suddenly there came a tapping," head slowly rising, eyes wandering to left, then to right; on last line both hands pass outward and down to side, face front.

2

"Ah, distinctly I remember, it was in the bleak Decem-
    ber,"

Transition—hands to lower zone, front, near body, fingers loosely interlocked, head drooped, face sad.

3

"And each separate dying ember wrought its ghost upon the floor."

Pos. 4—(narrow.) Transition—hands pass to upper zone, front, then outward and into middle zone, oblique front, palms vertical, eyes looking toward oblique left, forward and downward, body somewhat retreated.

4

"Eagerly I wished the morrow:"

Transition—hands pass outward and float down to side.

5

"Vainly I had sought to borrow
From my books surcease of sorrow—"

Line of gravity to left foot. Transition—hands pass inward from side to lower zone, front, then to upper zone and outward and slowly downward again, making one complete circle.

6

"Sorrow for the lost Lenore—
For the rare and radiant maiden whom the angels name Lenore—"

Transition—hands from lower zone to upper zone, front, palms supine on "Lost Lenore" and held until last line, when the movement is repeated in upper zone, and hands pass to oblique front, head and eyes raised.

7

"Nameless here forevermore."

Line of gravity to right foot. Transition—hands pass outward, palms upward, then float down to side, head dropped.

8

"And the silken, sad, uncertain rustling of each purple
 curtain,
Thrill'd me—filled me with fantastic terrors never felt
 before;
So that now, to still the beating of my heart, I stood
 repeating,
' 'Tis some visitor entreating entrance at my chamber-
 door,—
Some late visitor entreating entrance at my chamber-
 door;
  That it is, and nothing more.'"

Pos. 6. Transition—hands to upper zone, front, then outward, downward, and inward, one wrist upon the other, fingers clutching chest, shoulders drawn inward as in fear, body somewhat retreated, head forward, eyes anxious—hold attitude to end of stanza.

9

"Presently my soul grew stronger: hesitating then no
    longer,"

Line of gravity slowly shifted to left foot, body becoming more erect.

10

"'Sir,' said I, 'or Madam, truly your forgiveness I implore;'

Pos. 2.—Body bowing low as in courtesy. Transition—hands pass to upper zone, then downward and inward, crossing in front of waist, then to lower zone, lateral, palms facing front.

11

"'But the fact is, I was napping, and so gently you
    came rapping,
And so faintly you came tapping, tapping at my chamber-door,'

Pos. 3. Hands pass to front of waist, right hand crossing above left, and then forward to right oblique front, palm supine, left hand to lower zone, lateral, palm prone, face looking to oblique front, right; on the word "Tapping" right hand should be changed to vertical position and gently moved as in act of tapping a door.

12

"'That I scarce was sure I heard you—'"

Transition—hands to middle zone, front, passing to oblique front, palms supine.

13

"Here I open'd wide the door:"

Line of gravity to left foot. Transition—hands in toward chest, then right hand to lateral, palm vertical, left hand at same time passing to lower zone, lateral, palm prone.

14

"Darkness there, and nothing more."

Transition—hands pass into upper zone, over head, then outward, palms vertical; face expressive of astonishment.

15

"Deep into that darkness peering, long I stood there, wondering, fearing,
Doubting, dreaming dreams no mortals ever dared to dream before;"

Line of gravity to right foot, but returning to left foot on "Fearing" and retained. Transition—hands pass down and in toward front of waist, then higher and well forward with palms vertical and fingers separated; on "Fearing," hands are brought inward toward chest, then outward and downward in middle zone, oblique front, palms supine on "Doubting" and held.

16

" But the silence was unbroken, and the stillness gave no token,"

Transition—hands to upper zone, front, crossing one above the other, then outward, palms vertical, moving downward to middle zone, lateral, on " Stillness," etc.

17

"And the only word there spoken was the whisper'd word, ' Lenore !' "

Line of gravity slowly to right foot. Transition— hands toward front of chest, then right hand slightly forward, left hand to midde zone, lateral, palm of each vertical.

18

"This I whisper'd, and an echo murmur'd back the word, ' LENORE !'
Merely this, and nothing more."

Line of gravity slowly to left foot. Transition— right hand in toward left chest, left hand lowered, palm prone, then both hands to front and downward on last face toward oblique front, right.

19

" Back into the chamber turning, all my soul within me burning,"

Pos. 4—with head and chest turned oblique back,

right. Transition—hands passing toward front of waist, then forward oblique back, right, right hand more extended than left, palms facing, eyes following.

20

"Soon again I heard a tapping, something louder than before."

Right hand toward right ear as if listening, left hand with fingers near right shoulder, palm front, head gradually turned to left oblique, eyes looking out over left shoulder and somewhat upward.

21

"'Surely,' said I, 'surely that is something at my window-lattice;'

Pos. 1—Slowly and on last part of line. Transition —hands to upper zone, then outward and in to front, not far from shoulders, elbows slightly bent and outward, palms vertical, head and eyes toward left oblique forward.

22

"'Let me see then what thereat is, and this mystery explore,—'

Same as preceding, except hands pass outward toward lateral.

23

"'Let my heart be still a moment, and this mystery explore;—
       Tis the wind, and nothing more.'"

Transition—hands downward and inward to lower zone, front, then placed on heart, one above the other, elbows well out, body a little more erect, eyes slowly wandering.

24

"Open here I flung the shutter,"

Transition—hands to front with palms vertical and passing quickly to lateral.

25

"When with many a flirt and flutter,
In there stepped a stately raven of the saintly days of yore."

Hands higher on first line, face showing astonishment; for second line: Pos. 6. Transition—hands crossing near front of chest, right hand to front, palm supine, finger tips directed downward, left hand to middle zone, lateral, palm prone, eyes to front and downward.

26

"Not the least obeisance made he; not a minute stopp'd or stay'd he;

Right hand—repeating preceding gesture on "Least obeisance."

27

"But, with mien of lord or lady, perch'd above my chamber-door,—"

Pos. 6. Transition—right hand toward left shoulder, then to upper zone, right oblique forward, palm supine, eyes following.

28

"Perch'd upon a bust of Pallas, just above my chamber-door—
    Perched and sat and nothing more."

Transition—right hand inward toward chest, then to preceding position, index finger strong, palm prone.

29

"Then this ebony bird beguiling my sad fancy into smiling,
By the grave and stern decorum of the countenance it wore,
'Though thy crest be shorn and shaven, thou,' I said, 'art sure no craven;
Ghastly, grim, and ancient raven, wandering from the nightly shore,
Tell me what thy lordly name is on the Night's Plutonian shore?'"

Line of gravity to left foot, body well drawn up, arms folded, head and eyes upward, oblique front, right.

30

"Quoth the raven, 'Nevermore!'"

Transition—arms unfolding, hands passing to upper zone front, and floating outward and downward to side, face front.

31

"Much I marvel'd this ungainly fowl to hear discourse
 so plainly,
Though its answer little meaning—little relevancy
 bore;"

Pos. 5. Transition—hands upward to middle zone, front, then to oblique front, palms vertical.

32

"For we cannot help agreeing that no living human
 being
Ever yet was blessed with seeing bird above his chamber-door—"

Transition—hands passing inward, then outward to same position, palms supine.

33

"Bird or beast upon the sculptured bust above his
 chamber-door,
 With such name as 'Nevermore!'"

Transition—right hand inward, then to upper zone, oblique front, right, pointing with index finger, left hand down to side.

34

"But the raven still beguiling all my sad soul into
 smiling,"

Line of gravity to left foot. Transition—hands to upper zone, and slowly descending to side, face front.

35
"Straight I wheel'd a cushion'd seat in front of bird, and bust, and door."

Swing body well over on left foot on "Straight," then to Pos. 3. Transition—hands to middle zone, oblique back, left, then forward to oblique front, right, palms prone, eyes following, looking upward on "Bird," etc.

36
"Then, upon the velvet sinking, I betook myself to linking
Fancy unto fancy, thinking what this ominous bird of yore—
What this grim, ungainly, ghastly, gaunt, and ominous bird of yore
Meant in croaking 'Nevermore!'"

Transition—hands to upper zone front, then outward and downward into lower zone near body, one index finger linked in the other, head and eyes dropped as if in deep meditation.

37
"This I sat engaged in guessing, but no syllable expressing"

Transition—right hand to upper zone, oblique front, right, index finger strong, palm vertical, head and eyes in same direction, left hand to lower zone lateral, palm prone.

38

"To the fowl, whose fiery eyes now burn'd into my bosom's core;"

Line of gravity to left foot. Transition—right hand with index finger and thumb strongly against left side of chest, face expressive of strong feeling.

39

"This and more I sat divining, with my head at ease reclining
On the cushion's velvet lining that the lamp-light gloated o'er,"

Transition—hands pass to upper zone front, then outward and downward to lower zone, and loosely clasped in front of dress, body, head, and eyes drooped.

40

"But whose velvet violet lining, with the lamp-light gloating o'er,"

Head and eyes slowly rising on last part of line.

41

"She shall press—ah! nevermore!"

Hands strongly clasped and brought to chest, elbows high, head back, eyes up; hands still clasped rising high into upper zone on "Ah!" then forward and down into lower zone close to body, head and eyes dropped.

42

"Then methought the air grew denser, perfumed from an unseen censer"

Pos. 5—(narrow.) Transition—hands upward to front of chest, then outward to lateral, palms supine, face front.

43

"Swung by seraphim, whose foot-falls tinkled on the tufted floor."

Transition—on first part of line, carry right hand over to left side, then both hands swung over to right side, palms prone, then on "Tinkled," etc., both hands moving with light, tripping motion to front, eyes following.

44

"'Wretch,' I cried, 'thy God hath lent thee—by these angels He hath sent thee
Respite—respite and nepenthe'

Transition—hands pass slightly upward, then in on chest, one hand upon the other, head and eyes raised, body strongly drawn up.

45

"'From thy memories of Lenore!'

Transition—hands slowly passing outward to oblique front, palms supine.

46

"'Quaff, oh, quaff this kind nepenthe, and forget this lost Lenore!'"

Transition—hands slowly inward, then clasping head, elbows well out.

47

"Quoth the raven, 'Nevermore!'"

Line of gravity to left foot. Transition—hands above head, then outward and downward to side, head and eyes lowered.

48

"'Prophet!' said I, 'thing of evil!—prophet still, if bird or devil!'"

Pos. 2—(narrow.) Transition—right hand upward and inward toward chest, then to upper zone, oblique front, palm supine, head upward toward oblique right, astonished expression.

49

"'Whether tempter sent, or whether tempest toss'd thee here ashore,'"

Body well drawn up. Transition—right hand high above head, then by straight-line arm movement to lower zone near body, index finger pointing downward, left hand still in lower zone, palm prone; on "Tempest tossed," etc., right hand toward left hip, then both hands oblique front, right, a little above middle zone, palms prone.

50

"'Desolate, yet all undaunted, on this desert land enchanted—'"

Transition—hands to upper zone, front, then outward and downward, lateral, palms prone on "Desolate," hands in fists on "Undaunted," body drawn up, then opening hands and relaxing body on rest of line.

51

"'On this home by Horror haunted—'"

Body drawn backward. Transition—right hand near forehead, palm front, elbow well out, left hand in lower zone, lateral and clinched.

52

"'Tell me truly, I implore—'"

Pos. 3. Transition—hands passing near waist, then right hand to upper zone, right oblique, front, palm supine, left to lower zone, oblique back, left, palm prone.

53

"'Is there—is there balm in Gilead?—'"

Transition—right hand in toward left shoulder, then high into upper zone, index finger strong.

54
" ' Tell me—tell me, I implore!' "

Transition—right hand downward and outward, then inward, meeting left hand near chest, then both to upper zone, oblique right, strongly forward and clasped.

55
" Quoth the raven, ' Nevermore!' "

Line of gravity to left foot. Transition—hands outward, descending to side, face front, head downward.

56
" ' Prophet,' said I, ' thing of evil!—prophet still, if bird or devil!'

Line of gravity to right foot. Transition—hands to middle zone, front, then right hand passing to oblique front, palm vertical, left hand to lower zone, lateral, well extended, palm prone, head and eyes upward, oblique front, right.

57
" ' By that heaven that bends above us—by that God we both adore,'

Transition—hands pass to front of waist, then into upper zone over head, separating and descending on first part of line, then upward through middle zone, front, to upper zone, front, palms supine, on last clause.

58

"'Tell this soul, with sorrow laden, if, within the distant Aidenn,
It shall clasp a sainted maiden, whom the angels name Lenore;'

Transition—hands outward and downward, then crossed at wrists over chest, eyes and head strongly raised, whole manner imploring.

59

"'Clasp a rare and radiant maiden,'

Transition—arms still crossed at wrists, but hands slowly rising from chest.

60

"'Whom the angels name Lenore!'
Quoth the raven, 'Nevermore!'"

Transition—hands to upper zone, oblique front, palms supine on first line, then outward and downward to side on second line.

61

"'Be that word our sign of parting, bird or fiend!' I shriek'd, upstarting—"

Pos. 2. Transition—hands quickly to upper zone front, palms vertical, fingers somewhat separated, face indicative of horror.

62

"'Get thee back into the tempest and the Night's Plutonian shore!'

Body firm. Transition—hands in fists by straight-line arm movement, to lower zone, lateral.

63

"'Leave no black plume as a token of that lie thy soul hath spoken!'

Pos. 3. Transition—right hand carried high over head, then by straight-line arm movement to lower zone, oblique right, palm supine, and firmly held.

64

"'Leave my loneliness unbroken!—'

Body and head inclined slightly to left and relaxed, palms prone, hands slowly falling.

65

"'Quit the bust above my door!'

Body strongly drawn up. Transition—hands to middle zone, front, right crossing above left and passing by strong straight-line arm movement to upper zone, oblique front, index finger very straight, palm vertical, left at same time to lower zone, oblique back, hand in fist.

66

"'Take thy beak from out my heart,'

Line of gravity to left foot. Transition—hands to middle zone, front, and in toward heart, fingers spread and contracted, palms vertical, elbows well out, countenance that of horrified determination.

67

"'And take thy form off my door!'"

Hands in fists rise convulsively over head, palm part upward, elbows outward.

68

"Quoth the raven, 'Nevermore!'"

"And the raven, never flitting, still is sitting, still is sitting
On the pallid bust of Pallas, just above my chamber-door;"

Body relaxed. Transition—hands very slowly moving higher, then floating outward and downward to side, head drooping.

69

"And his eyes have all the seeming of a demon's that is dreaming,"

Body drawn toward oblique back, left. Transition—hands from lower zone, in toward chest, then right hand to oblique front, right, above line of shoulder, elbow slightly outward and backward, left hand in front of right shoulder, palms of both vertical, head turned toward oblique left, eyes toward oblique right, face, strongly expressive.

70

"And the lamp-light o'er him streaming throws his shadow on the floor;"

Pos. 5—(narrow.) Transition—hands to upper zone, front, then outward, descending to middle zone, front, palms prone on first part of line, then inward and outward and downward on remainder of line, head up on first part, downward on last.

71

"And my soul from out that shadow that lies floating on the floor"

Transition—hands to lower zone, front, palms prone.

72

"Shall be lifted—NEVERMORE."

Transition—hands from lower zone, front, to upper zone, front, on first part of line, head also rising, then descending to lower zone, head drooped, expression that of despair.

SUGGESTION

The following is a list of musical selections suitable, in part or whole, for Pantomimic action:

1. The Two Angels, ... *Blumenthal*
    (Arranged by A. W. Berg.)
2. The Last Hope, ... *Gottschalk.*
3. The Hundredth Psalm, ... *Wm. V. Wallace.*
4. Improvisation—Op. 48, No. 2, ... *S. Jadassohn.*
5. Marcia Fantastica—Op. 31, ... *W. Bargiel.*
6. Variations of Home Sweet Home.
7. Amaryllis, ... *Ghys.*
8. The Nocturne and The Wedding March of The Midsummer Night's Dream, ... *Mendelssohn.*
    (Arranged by Sidney Smith.)
9. The Funeral March of a Marionette, ... *Chas. Gounod.*
10. The Swing Song, ... *Fontaine.*
11. Acht Skizzen, ... *Arthur Bird.*
12. The Monastery Bells.
13. The Musical Box—Op. 19, ... *E. Liebach.*
14. The Joyful Peasant, ... *Schumann, Op. 68, No. 9.*
    (Arranged by A. Hartl.)
15. Bright Star of Hope—Op. 51, ... *Theo. G. Boettger.*
16. Serenade, ... *Schubert.*
    (Transcription—A. Loumey.)

"Quaff, oh, quaff this kind nepenthe,
And forget this lost Lenore!"

17. The Monk's Prayer, ...*Julius E. Müller.*
18. The Miserere and Prison Scene from Il Trovatore—Op. 39, No. 3, ... *Edouard Dorn.*
19. Bonnie Sweet Bessie—Op. 75, ... *T. P. Ryder.*
20. Berceuse, ... *Josef Hofmann.*

The following-named hymns and songs can also be used with good effect:

1. "Abide with Me, Fast Falls the Eventide."
2. Nearer, My God, to Thee.
3. Almost Persuaded.
4. Fading, Still Fading.
5. Softly Now the Light of Day.
6. The Star-Spangled Banner.
7. Robin Adair.
8. I Dreamt I Dwelt in Marble Halls.
9. Juanita.
10. Last Rose of Summer.

SHOEMAKER'S
Best Selections
FOR
READINGS AND RECITATIONS

Numbers 1 to 19 Now Issued

Paper binding, each number, - 30 cents
Cloth   "   "   "   - 50   "

☞ SPECIAL.—For a limited time we offer the full set of 19 numbers, in paper binding, at the special price of $3.80, and in cloth binding at $6.35.

This series was formerly called "The Elocutionist's Annual," the first 17 numbers being published under that title. The change in name is made because it is believed a more appropriate title is thus secured.

Teachers, Readers, Students, and all persons who have occasion to use books of this kind, concede this to be the best series of speakers published. The different numbers are compiled by leading elocutionists of the country, who have exceptional facilities for securing selections, and whose judgment as to their merits is invaluable. No trouble or expense is spared to obtain the very best readings and recitations, and much material is used by special arrangement with other publishers, thus securing the best selections from such American authors as Longfellow, Holmes, Whittier, Lowell, Emerson, Alice and Phœbe Cary, Mrs. Stowe, and many others. The foremost English authors are also represented, as well as the leading French and German writers.

Sold by all Booksellers and Newsdealers, or mailed upon receipt of price.

THE PENN PUBLISHING COMPANY
1020 Arch Street
Philadelphia

Practical Elocution

By J. W. SHOEMAKER, A. M.

300 PAGES, CLOTH, LEATHER BACK, $1.25

This work is the outgrowth of actual class-room experience, and is a practical, common-sense treatment of the whole subject. It is clear and concise, yet comprehensive, and is absolutely free from the entangling technicalities that are so frequently found in books of this class. It advocates no individual system, but appeals to the intelligence of any ordinary mind, and it can therefore be as successfully used by the average teacher of reading, as by the trained elocutionist.

Conversation, which is the basis of all true Elocution, is regarded as embracing all the germs of speech and action. Prominent attention is therefore given to the cultivation of this the most common form of human expression.

General principles and practical processes are presented for the cultivation of strength, purity, and flexibility of Voice, for the improvement of distinctness and correctness in Articulation, and for the development of Soul Power in delivery.

The work includes a systematic treatment of Gesture in its several departments of position, facial expression, and bodily movement, a brief system of Gymnastics bearing upon vocal development and grace of movement, and also a chapter on Methods of Instruction, for teachers.

Liberal discount for introduction and in quantity.

Sold by all Booksellers, or by

THE PENN PUBLISHING COMPANY
1020 Arch Street
Philadelphia

The Story of the Iliad

FOR BOYS AND GIRLS

By Dr. Edward Brooks, A. M.

370 Pages, Cloth, Illustrated, — — — **$1.25**

This is a story of absorbing interest both to young and old. It relates in a simple prose narrative the leading incidents of the greatest literary work of the world—the Iliad of Homer. Many of its names are household words among educated people, and its incidents are a constant source of allusion and illustration among the best speakers and writers. No one with any claim to literary culture can afford to be ignorant of them.

Dr. Brooks, its author, is one of the most distinguished educators and authors of the country, and his name attached to any work is a guarantee of its high merit. His style as an author is noted for its clearness and simplicity, and this admirable quality he has employed to the fullest extent in the present work, thus rendering the hidden beauties of this great literary production so plain and simple that they are within the comprehension of any boy or girl.

The mechanical execution of the book is the best, and the thirteen full-page illustrations found in it are exact copies of the celebrated Flaxman designs.

Sold by all booksellers, or mailed upon receipt of price.

THE PENN PUBLISHING COMPANY
1020 Arch Street
Philadelphia

THE
Story of the Odyssey
FOR BOYS AND GIRLS
BY DR. EDWARD BROOKS, A. M.

370 Pages, Cloth, Illustrated,   - - $1.25

A COMPANION volume to the "Story of the Iliad," being a simple prose narrative in the author's inimitable style.

The Odyssey has been a rich mine of wealth for poets and romancers, painters and sculptors, from the dim date of the age which we call Homer's down to our own. In this wonderful poem lie the germs of thousands of volumes which fill our modern libraries. Not that all their authors are willful plagiarists, or even conscious imitators; but because the Greek poet, first of all whose thoughts have been preserved to us in writing, touched, in their deepest as well as their lightest tones, those chords of human action and passion which find an echo in all hearts and in all ages.

Contains eighteen full-page illustrations of the Flaxman drawings.

Sold by all booksellers, or mailed upon receipt of price.

THE PENN PUBLISHING COMPANY
1020 Arch Street
Philadelphia

www.ingramcontent.com/pod-product-compliance
Lightning Source LLC
Chambersburg PA
CBHW020247170426
43202CB00008B/264